YORK NOTES

A CHRISTMAS CAROL

CHARLES DICKENS

NOTES BY LUCY ENGLISH

PEARSON

YORK PRESS

The right of Lucy English to be identified as Author of this Work has been asserted by her in accordance with the Copyright, Designs and Patents Act 1988

YORK PRESS
322 Old Brompton Road, London SW5 9JH

PEARSON EDUCATION LIMITED
Edinburgh Gate, Harlow,
Essex CM20 2JE, United Kingdom
Associated companies, branches and representatives throughout the world

First published 2015

10 9 8 7 6

ISBN 978–1–4479–8212–8

Illustrations by Kay Dixey; and Alan Batley (p. 61 only)

Phototypeset by Swales and Willis Ltd

Printed in China by Golden Cup

Photo credits: chrisbrignell/Thinkstock for page 8 top/Alexander Raths/ Shutterstock for page 9 middle/Vitalez/Shutterstock for page 10 bottom/ Romiana Lee/Shutterstock for page 11 bottom/Shelli Jensen/Shutterstock page 15 middle/Edward Westmacott/Shutterstock for page 16 top/ susandaniels/Thinkstock for page 17 middle/Africa Studio/Shutterstock for page 18 middle/Lightboxx/Shutterstock for page 19 bottom/ Dennis W. Donohue/Shutterstock for page 20 bottom/Paul Orr/Shutterstock for page 23 middle/Jeerawut Rityakul/Shutterstock for page 24 middle/ Kokhanchikov/Shutterstock for page 26 middle/Lakeview Images/ Shutterstock for page 27 bottom/© iStock/tataks for page 28 middle/ C. Byatt-Norman/Shutterstock for page 30 bottom/© iStock/Peeterv for page 35 middle/bikeriderlondon/Shutterstock for page 41 bottom/ Khomulo Anna/Shutterstock for page 42 bottom/Roman Bodnarchuk/ Shutterstock for page 43 bottom/jps/Shutterstock for page 48 bottom/ Balonici/Shutterstock for page 49 bottom/F9photos/Shutterstock for page 55 top/Kenny1/Shutterstock for page 56 bottom/Kuttelvaserova Stuchelova/ Shutterstock for page 59 bottom/Frannyanne/Shutterstock for page 60 bottom/Andrey Yurlov/Shutterstock for page 64 top/Everett Historical/ Shutterstock for page 65 top/yavuzunlu/Shutterstock for page 71 bottom/ wavebreakmedia/Shutterstock for page 79 middle

CONTENTS

PART ONE:
GETTING STARTED

Preparing for assessment...5

How to use your York Notes Study Guide 6

PART TWO:
PLOT AND ACTION

Plot summary...8

Preface...10

Stave One 11

Stave Two 19

Stave Three..28

Stave Four..34

Stave Five 40

Progress and revision check...44

PART THREE:
CHARACTERS

Who's who?..46

Marley's Ghost...47

Ebenezer Scrooge 48

Fred 50

Bob Cratchit...51

The Ghosts of Christmas 52

Progress and revision check...54

PART FOUR:
THEMES, CONTEXTS AND SETTINGS

Themes..55

Contexts..59

Settings...61

Progress and revision check...63

PART FIVE:
FORM, STRUCTURE AND LANGUAGE

Form 64

Structure 64

Language 65

Progress and revision check 69

PART SIX:
PROGRESS BOOSTER ★

Understanding the question 70

Planning your answer 70

Responding to writers' effects 72

Using quotations...74

Spelling, punctuation and grammar...75

Annotated sample answers...76

   Sample answer 1 76

   Sample answer 2 78

   Sample answer 3 80

Practice task...82

Further questions 82

PART SEVEN:
FURTHER STUDY AND ANSWERS

Literary terms 83

Checkpoint answers 84

Progress and revision check answers 85

Mark scheme 88

PREPARING FOR ASSESSMENT

HOW WILL I BE ASSESSED ON MY WORK ON *A CHRISTMAS CAROL*?

All exam boards are different but whichever course you are following, your work will be examined through these four Assessment Objectives:

Assessment Objectives	Wording	Worth thinking about ...
AO1	Read, understand and respond to texts. Students should be able to: ● maintain a critical style and develop an informed personal response ● use textual references, including quotations, to support and illustrate interpretations.	● How well do I know what happens, what people say, do etc? ● What do *I* think about the key ideas in the **novella**? ● How can I support my viewpoint in a really convincing way? ● What are the best quotations to use and when should I use them?
AO2	Analyse the language, form and structure used by a writer to create meanings and effects, using relevant subject terminology where appropriate.	● What specific things does the writer 'do'? What choices has Dickens made (why this particular word, phrase or paragraph here? Why does this event happen at this point?) ● What effects do these choices create? Suspense? **Ironic** laughter? Reflective mood?
AO3	Show understanding of the relationships between texts and the contexts in which they were written.	● What can I learn about society from the book? (What does it tell me about poverty and inequality in Dickens's day, for example?) ● What was society like in Dickens's time? Can I see it reflected in the story?
AO4	Use a range of vocabulary and sentence structures for clarity, purpose and effect, with accurate spelling and punctuation.	● How accurately and clearly do I write? ● Are there small errors of grammar, spelling and punctuation I can get rid of?

Look out for the Assessment Objective labels throughout your York Notes Study Guide – these will help to focus your study and revision!

The text used in this Study Guide is the New Windmills edition, 1992.

HOW TO USE YOUR YORK NOTES STUDY GUIDE

You are probably wondering what is the best and most efficient way to use your York Notes Study Guide on *A Christmas Carol*. Here are three possibilities:

A step-by-step study and revision guide	A 'dip-in' support when you need it	A revision guide after you have finished the novella
Step 1: Read Part Two as you read the novella as a companion to help you study it. **Step 2:** When you need to, turn to Parts Three to Five to focus your learning. **Step 3:** Then, when you have finished, use Parts Six and Seven to hone your exam skills, revise and practise for the exam.	Perhaps you know the book quite well, but you want to check your understanding and practise your exam skills? Just look for the section which you think you need most help with and go for it!	You might want to use the Notes after you have finished your study, using Parts Two to Five to check over what you have learned, and then work through Parts Six and Seven in the immediate weeks leading up to your exam.

HOW WILL THE GUIDE HELP YOU STUDY AND REVISE?

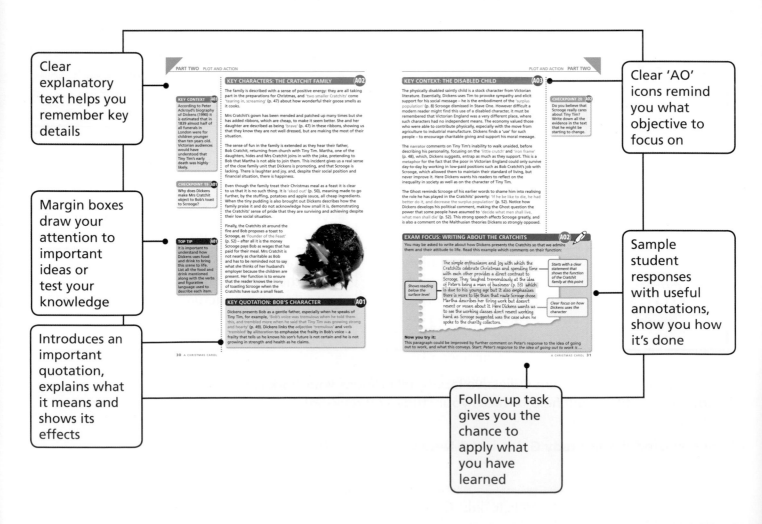

Clear explanatory text helps you remember key details

Margin boxes draw your attention to important ideas or test your knowledge

Introduces an important quotation, explains what it means and shows its effects

Clear 'AO' icons remind you what objective to focus on

Sample student responses with useful annotations, show you how it's done

Follow-up task gives you the chance to apply what you have learned

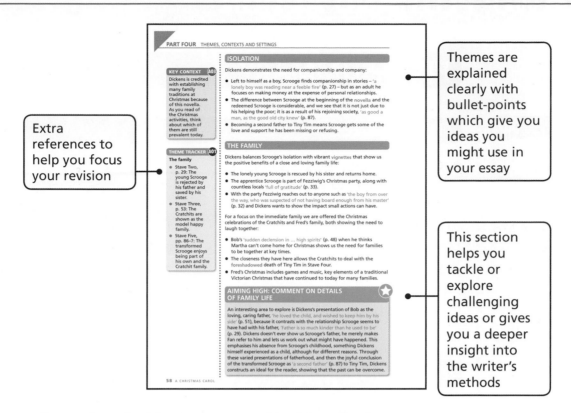

Extra references to help you focus your revision

Themes are explained clearly with bullet-points which give you ideas you might use in your essay

This section helps you tackle or explore challenging ideas or gives you a deeper insight into the writer's methods

Parts **Two** to **Five** each end with a **Progress and Revision Check**:

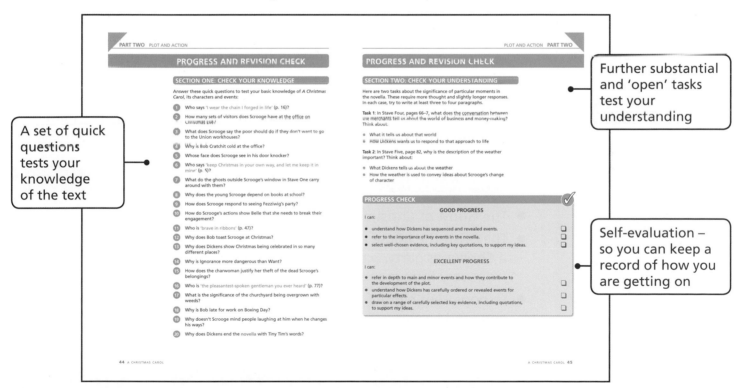

A set of quick questions tests your knowledge of the text

Further substantial and 'open' tasks test your understanding

Self-evaluation – so you can keep a record of how you are getting on

Don't forget **Parts Six** and **Seven**, with advice and practice on **improving your writing skills**:

- Focus on **difficult areas** such as **'context'** and **'inferences'**
- **Short snippets** of **other students' work** to show you how it's done (or not done!)
- Three annotated **sample responses** to a task **at different levels**, with **expert comments**, to help you judge your own level
- **Practice questions**
- **Answers** to the **Progress and Revision Checks** and **Checkpoint** margin boxes

Now it's up to you! Don't forget – there's even more help on our website with more sample answers, essay planners and even online tutorials. Go to **www.yorknotes.com** to find out more.

PLOT SUMMARY

THE PREFACE

- Charles Dickens writes a note to his readers to explain that he wants to introduce an entertaining idea to them.

STAVE ONE: MARLEY'S GHOST

- The reader is introduced to Ebenezer Scrooge who only cares about making money. It is Christmas Eve and he won't pay to heat the office properly. This means that his clerk, Bob Cratchit, is very cold.
- Scrooge has four Christmas visitors: his nephew, Fred; two charity collectors; and a carol singer. Scrooge is rude to all of them and sends them away.
- That night the Ghost of Jacob Marley, his dead business partner, appears. He tells Scrooge that his mean way of life will lead to misery and that three Ghosts will visit him to show him the error of his ways.

STAVE TWO: THE FIRST OF THE THREE SPIRITS

- The Ghost of Christmas Past shows Scrooge his unhappy childhood.
- They visit the house of Scrooge's first employer, Fezziwig, who is holding a Christmas party. Scrooge notices how much happiness can be obtained from very little money.
- Scrooge sees himself as a young man with Belle, the woman he was engaged to marry. Belle breaks off the engagement because she thinks Scrooge loves money more than he loves her.

STAVE THREE: THE SECOND OF THE THREE SPIRITS

- The Ghost of Christmas Present takes Scrooge to visit Christmas preparations at the Cratchits' house. Scrooge learns that Tiny Tim will not survive unless the future changes. This knowledge upsets Scrooge.
- The Ghost takes Scrooge to see different groups of people enjoying themselves at Christmas. Scrooge sees his nephew, Fred, with his family. They are discussing Scrooge and Fred is full of pity for him.
- At the end of the night the Ghost shows Scrooge two children: a boy, called Ignorance, and a girl, called Want. The Ghost says they belong to Man and warns Scrooge to beware of them both, but especially to beware of Ignorance.

STAVE FOUR: THE LAST OF THE SPIRITS

- The mysterious Ghost of Christmas Yet to Come takes Scrooge into the future to witness different conversations about a dead man. No one cares that this man has died, and the thieves have so little respect that they have stolen the clothes from his corpse.
- In contrast, the Ghost then takes Scrooge to see the Cratchits who are deeply upset because Tiny Tim has died.
- Finally, Scrooge is shown a gravestone with his own name on it. He realises he is the dead man whom the people were talking about. He promises to change his ways.

STAVE FIVE: THE END OF IT

- Waking up in his own bed, back in the present, Scrooge is delighted to be given a second chance and makes Christmas happy for everyone. He sends a turkey to the Cratchits, gives money to the charity collectors, and joins Fred for Christmas. The next day he raises Bob's wages and promises to become a friend to Tiny Tim, who does not die.

KEY CONTEXT **A03**

Dickens toured America reading *A Christmas Carol* to audiences. One observer at a reading said Tiny Tim's death 'brought out so many pocket handkerchiefs that it looked as if a snow-storm had somehow gotten into the hall without tickets' (reported by Michael Patrick Hearn in *The Annotated Christmas Carol* (2003)).

REVISION FOCUS: MAKING SURE YOU KNOW THE PLOT

It is important that you know all the key events in the novella so that you can make reference to them if needed in the exam. Create a visual reminder chart to make sure you know what happens and when. Either draw images or print them from an internet image search to create a page for each Stave. When you have finished, cover them up and see if you can remember each one. Keep testing yourself until you know exactly what happened in each Stave.

THE PREFACE: CHARLES DICKENS'S MESSAGE

SUMMARY

- Dickens speaks directly to his readers and tells us that his story has a key idea behind it.
- He hopes his readers will not be offended by this idea and will adopt it themselves.

WHY IS THIS SECTION IMPORTANT?

A It tells his readers that Dickens is going to be the narrator of this story.

B He wants us to think seriously about the **message** in the book.

C The **theme of ghosts** is introduced.

TOP TIP: WRITING ABOUT STYLE

It is important that you can write about Dickens's style. Here he over-uses the semantic field of the supernatural to establish the subject matter of the novella and to show us that it's not intended to be frightening. He calls the novella a 'Ghostly little book' and refers to his 'Ghost of an Idea'. This makes the idea sound insubstantial and harmless, and certainly not threatening. Dickens wants his ideas to 'haunt' the 'house' of the reader – the house in this case is not just the reader's home, but also their body and mind.

Dickens wants the reader to accept and embrace the ideas in this book, and not just dismiss them when they finish reading it. He also uses the term 'lay', which can mean to put away. When used in relation to ghosts, however, it means to exorcise a ghost, or stop one appearing. These puns set the tone of this story and show it is meant to entertain as well as convey his message.

STAVE ONE, PAGES 1–3: MARLEY IS DEAD AND SCROOGE CARES ONLY ABOUT MONEY

SUMMARY

- We learn that Jacob Marley was Scrooge's business partner but has been dead for seven years.
- Scrooge was the only person at Marley's funeral but immediately after it he went back to work.
- Scrooge hasn't painted out Marley's name on the sign and doesn't care if that causes confusion.
- All Scrooge cares about is making money.
- We are told that Scrooge is colder at heart than the winter weather.
- We first meet Scrooge on Christmas Eve. He is at work and it is very cold and foggy.

WHY IS THIS SECTION IMPORTANT?

A We need to know that **Marley is dead** so we believe in his ghost when it appears.

B Dickens uses the opening line to hint at the **supernatural story** to come: 'Marley was dead to begin with' (p. 1).

C Scrooge's **mean** and **harsh** nature is described.

D Dickens uses the **weather** to set the tone and reflect Scrooge's state of mind.

KEY THEME: LONELINESS AND ISOLATION (A02)

Dickens makes it very clear to us that Scrooge cares only about making money and doesn't have any friends; in fact even guide dogs avoid him. Scrooge was the only person directly affected by Marley's death but hasn't let this upset him at all. The repetition of 'sole' (p. 1) emphasises the fact that Marley was so focused on business he didn't have time for any other friends or family. It also makes us think of the spiritual 'soul'; something this novella is concerned with. This is developed by the **simile** 'solitary as an oyster' (p. 2) suggesting there might be something precious inside Scrooge (like a pearl) but it is closed up and protected against the world.

TOP TIP (A02)

It is important to understand how Dickens emphasises Scrooge's cold and harsh character through the language he uses. Go through these pages and list each aspect Dickens tells us about.

CHECKPOINT 2 (A02)

What is the impact of listing so many negative descriptions of Scrooge?

STAVE ONE, PAGES 3–10: SCROOGE HAS VISITORS AT THE OFFICE

SUMMARY

- Scrooge doesn't trust his assistant, Bob Cratchit, and keeps an eye on him at work.
- The office is very cold because Scrooge won't spend money on heating it.
- Fred, Scrooge's nephew, comes to wish Scrooge a merry Christmas but Scrooge calls him a fool for being happy when he doesn't have much money.
- Two charity collectors ask Scrooge for money to help the poor. Scrooge is rude to them and says the poor should either go to the Workhouse or die.
- The weather gets even worse and we are told a church bell can just be seen through the fog, looking down on Scrooge.
- Away from the office lots of people are having fun getting ready for Christmas.
- Reluctantly, Scrooge says Bob Cratchit may have Christmas Day off.
- Bob goes home in a playful mood and slides on the snow. This contrasts with Scrooge, who follows his usual routine and walks through the dark to his 'gloomy' (p. 10) home.

WHY IS THIS SECTION IMPORTANT?

A We learn just how **unpleasant** Scrooge is to everyone he encounters.

B The **'problem of the poor'** is introduced and we are reminded that not everyone has fun at Christmas.

C We can see what Bob Cratchit **experiences** in his job.

TOP TIP A01

Make sure you understand how Dickens uses the character of Fred to present an alternative way of living and treating others. Go through the novella and note all the times Dickens uses Fred. Ask yourself how his actions and language combine to convey Dickens's message.

CHECKPOINT 3 A01

What does the different behaviour of Scrooge and Cratchit on their way home tell us about their characters?

KEY LANGUAGE: PATHETIC FALLACY (A02)

The **narrator** introduces the **image** of Scrooge counting money, even though it is Christmas Eve. It is cold, and the fog is almost alive, 'pouring in at every chink and keyhole' (p. 3). This is an example of **pathetic fallacy** (a form of **personification**), where inanimate objects of nature such as the weather reflect human emotions – in this case, Scrooge's bad temper is made visible in the fog. The fact it is getting everywhere demonstrates how infectious negative emotions can be.

KEY CHARACTER: FRED (A02)

The atmosphere is transformed with the cheerful entrance of Scrooge's nephew, Fred. He has come to wish Scrooge a merry Christmas and represents all Scrooge is not. He is 'all in a glow' (p. 4) because he has been walking fast, and is happy. This also suggests that he has a warm personality, the opposite of Scrooge's. Fred doesn't allow himself to be disheartened by Scrooge's gruff replies, and stands up for himself and his beliefs even though Scrooge calls him a fool. As well as providing a contrast with Scrooge in terms of character, we also learn that Fred does not have Scrooge's wealth – in fact, one of the reasons Scrooge calls Fred a fool is because he got married for love rather than money.

> **TOP TIP** (A02)
>
> It is important to understand how Dickens makes the weather worsen through this section. Draw a line that tracks how bad it is following Scrooge's words and actions.

EXAM FOCUS: WRITING ABOUT CHARACTER (A01)

You may be asked to write about how Dickens uses the supporting characters such as Fred. Read this example, commenting on how Fred provides a contrast to Scrooge:

> *Starts with a clear statement that shows Fred's function at this point*

Fred's enthusiasm and passion for the potential good Christmas can do is inspiring and highlights Scrooge's cold and unpleasant nature. Dickens uses Fred to remind us of our mortality, when he remarks that all people are 'fellow-passengers to the grave' (p. 5), which summarises the journey on which Scrooge is about to embark.

> *Clear focus on how Dickens uses Fred's character*

> *Good interpretation of character and meaning*

Fred's focus on togetherness and value that isn't merely monetary makes Scrooge seem very short-sighted in contrast and we question what he actually wants all his money for – it's not as if he enjoys it.

Now you try it:

This paragraph could be improved by further comment on the role of Fred. Add another sentence, picking up on the language Fred uses and its effect. Start: *Fred's use of language ...*

KEY THEME: RESPONSIBILITY FOR OTHERS (A03)

Dickens introduces his moral message through Scrooge's conversations with Fred and the charity collectors. Scrooge believes that financial profit is all that matters but his visitors provide the opposite argument. Fred states that men and women should 'open their shut-up hearts freely' (p. 5) and think of others as well as themselves, and the two 'portly gentlemen' (p. 6) ask Scrooge to give them some money to help 'the poor and destitute, who suffer greatly at the present time' (p. 7). Rather than give them money, Scrooge demands to know whether the prisons, the 'Union workhouses' and the 'Treadmill and the Poor Law' (p. 7) are still in operation. As far as he is concerned, these places are meant to provide for the poor and he doesn't see why he should contribute anything to them. He has to pay a tax to support these institutions, and he thinks that is enough.

However, the workhouses were well known for being hard and demeaning and the charity collectors point out that 'Many can't go there; and many would rather die' (p. 8). Here we see Scrooge's harsh and callous nature: he thinks if the poor would rather die they should hurry up and do so as that would 'decrease the surplus population' (p. 8). This is a disturbing idea to us, as Dickens intends it to be. He is presenting an accepted economic theory of the time, suggested by Thomas Malthus, and he wants us to reject it as we reject Scrooge's attitude to the poor.

KEY SETTING: OUTSIDE THE OFFICE (A02)

Away from Scrooge's office the atmosphere is very different; we are shown snapshots of people getting ready for the festive season – labourers gather together to enjoy a warming fire while traders display their goods with style. There are also carol singers on the street – but the singer who dares to stop outside Scrooge's door is rudely chased away by Scrooge.

Scrooge follows his usual routine on his journey home, showing that he is not willing to make any changes for Christmas. He eats by himself at a tavern, reads the newspapers and does some work. Finally, he walks home. He lives in 'a gloomy suite of rooms' (p. 10), stuck at the back of a dark and dreary yard. Dickens has gradually increased the fog and it is now so thick that Scrooge has to find his way with his hands; this physical loss of sight **metaphorically** highlights the emotional lack of understanding that Scrooge has about the meaning and value of life and how we should treat others.

KEY CONTEXT (A03)

Thomas Robert Malthus was an economist who predicted that food supplies and resources would never be enough for the whole population, meaning that poverty and hunger were inevitable for some. Dickens did not agree, as we can see from the way he invites us to reject Scrooge and his use of Malthus's theory (now thought to be incorrect).

CHECKPOINT 4 (A02)

Why does Dickens show us so many quick snapshots of people getting into the Christmas spirit?

STAVE ONE, PAGES 10–20: MARLEY'S GHOST HAS A MESSAGE FOR SCROOGE

SUMMARY

- When Scrooge gets to his front door, his door knocker changes into the face of his old business partner, Jacob Marley.

- Scrooge goes up to his rooms, checks them and then locks himself in.

- As Scrooge sits in front of his fire he hears bells ring and then Marley's Ghost appears. It is covered with chains of keys, padlocks and other items associated with the money-lending business he and Scrooge ran together.

- Marley explains that he is in torment because he only cared about money when he was alive and he now knows how wrong that was – he tells Scrooge that he should have cared about people.

- Marley's Ghost informs Scrooge that he will be visited by three more spirits.

- Scrooge doesn't want to think about what has happened and goes straight to bed.

WHY IS THIS SECTION IMPORTANT?

A We see that Scrooge is **strong-willed**: he resists believing that he is seeing and speaking to a ghost and tries to find **excuses** to explain it away.

B We learn that Marley **regrets** caring only about money and now sees he should have cared for people.

C The plot is set up: Scrooge will have **three more ghostly visitors** that night, all with the aim of saving him from Marley's fate of eternal regret.

KEY LANGUAGE: THE DOOR KNOCKER (A02)

Dickens devotes a whole paragraph to the description of Scrooge's door knocker, helping the reader to visualise it, but also ensuring that we understand its full significance – Scrooge isn't the sort of person who 'sees things' and Marley has been dead for years. The use of similes is rather unusual; the face has 'a dismal light about it, like a bad lobster in a dark cellar' (p. 11). This suggests it has a strange glow, indicating its otherworldliness.

As Scrooge looks at the face it becomes a knocker again, as if he had just imagined it. We are told he doesn't react, but he does look behind the door before closing it, as if he expected to find the back of Marley's head sticking out. The narrator emphasises this by the repeated use of italics when we are told Scrooge '*did* pause' and '*did* look' (p. 11). His expression of dismissal, 'Pooh, pooh!' (p. 11), is perhaps an indication that the sight has affected him, and he feels the need to verbally reject it. In this paragraph we see Dickens's careful choice of words – both in visual descriptions but also in how he presents Scrooge's reactions – all the time drawing the reader into the scene and what is happening.

KEY QUOTATION: SCROOGE'S CHARACTER (A01)

The narrator repeatedly emphasises that Scrooge isn't the type of person to imagine the ghostly events he is about to experience: 'Scrooge was not a man to be frightened by echoes' (p. 11). Dickens makes this statement of fact to encourage us to accept Marley and the other Ghosts as real, and not a figment of Scrooge's imagination. You could argue that the use of the word 'echoes' is ironic, however, as Scrooge is about to be haunted by past events.

KEY LANGUAGE: DICKENS'S USE OF SOUND (A02)

Dickens makes sure we know it is dark, reducing Scrooge's use of the sense of sight. This makes the use of sound even more effective.

The chilling atmosphere is extended by the description of the sound of the door closing. The noise 'resounded through the house like thunder' (p. 11), reminding us of the poor weather outside. It is not just the echo of the door closing that can be heard; all the bottles of wine in the cellars below 'have a separate peal of echoes' (p. 11). This reminds us of church bells ringing, a sound that will be heard throughout the novella signalling the arrival of each Ghost.

Before we see Marley's Ghost, Dickens uses sound to set up our expectations: there is 'a clanking noise deep down below' (Stave One, p. 13) and Scrooge remembers that ghosts drag chains. Dickens is careful to set this up before we see Marley to ensure we accept him as a ghost.

KEY CHARACTER: SCROOGE'S DETERMINED CHARACTER

Dickens helps us understand that Scrooge is strong-willed and determined, even when things aren't as he expects. He checks all his rooms, indicating he has been unsettled by what he has seen. He double-locks himself in, something we are told 'was not his custom' (p. 12), thus increasing our sense of unease. Dickens deliberately lists all the checks he makes; this list builds our knowledge of how Scrooge lives and our sense of nervousness and suspense – we know something is going to happen.

As well as being too mean to have a large fire at work, Scrooge is too mean to have a large one at home, and he has to sit near the fire to feel its warmth. The fireplace surround has decorated tiles with pictures of Bible stories, but when Scrooge looks at them all he can see is Marley's face. Scrooge refuses to believe it but still walks across the room to get away from the sight, showing us that the unflappable Scrooge is unnerved by what he has seen.

CHECKPOINT 7

Why is each Ghost always referred to as 'it'?

KEY QUOTATION: MARLEY'S TORMENT

Marley's Ghost tells Scrooge of the terrible situation it is in. Its punishment for being too concerned with making money when it was alive is to 'wander through the world – oh, woe is me! – and witness what [I] cannot share, but might have shared on earth, and turned to happiness!' (p. 16). The language used to support these ideas is strong. Words such as 'doomed', 'fettered' and 'ponderous' (p. 16) add to the sense of weight and make us take this message seriously. As Scrooge is being told of the Ghost's situation, so we are made to think of our own. The key message here is that happiness comes from helping and working with other people, not from making as much money as possible.

Look at Scrooge's behaviour at the end of Stave One. How do we know that he has been affected by what has happened?

KEY CONTEXT: THE 1834 NEW POOR LAW

Dickens makes a direct criticism of politics and the latest version of the Poor Law through Marley. At the end of its visit the Ghost opens the window and shows Scrooge the air full of tormented ghosts. The language used to describe this scene emphasises its misery and horror: the sounds are 'incoherent' and 'inexpressibly sorrowful' (p. 19). The ghosts are all suffering from being unable to help humans who are in need, something they didn't consider whilst they were alive but they now understand was key to their happiness and that of others. Dickens returns us to reality by making the political point that ghosts of 'guilty governments' (p. 20) are being made to suffer as a group for failing to help those in need.

TOP TIP **A01**

It is important to be clear about the order of events in the novella. Make sure you know the order of all the interactions that Scrooge has had in this Stave, from Fred arriving to wish him Merry Christmas to Marley's Ghost. Reread the whole Stave and write down the name of each character and what their interaction tells us about Scrooge.

AIMING HIGH: NARRATIVE TRICKS

If you want to show your understanding of the novella as a piece of fiction, it's important to be able to discuss the key role of Dickens as narrator. Dickens is rather an intrusive narrator and he manipulates and includes the reader throughout the novella. When the door knocker is introduced he draws our attention to it, emphasising the fact that there is nothing unusual about it except its large size. When it mysteriously changes into the face of Marley, Scrooge's dead business partner, the narrator again uses the first-person narrative to ask if any reader can explain why the knocker has changed. We tend to forget it is the author who makes a direct appeal to us in this way: it has a double effect of engaging us and making the events seem out of the narrator's control because he isn't able to explain them.

Dickens uses a similar narrative technique when we are made to imagine for ourselves the horrors Marley's Ghost is experiencing. By suggesting that the wailing sounds the ghosts make are beyond the narrator's description, readers have to use their imagination. Again, the scene is enhanced and enriched by our own ideas of how terrible these ghosts might sound. It is an example of Dickens inviting his audience/readership to participate in the story.

STAVE TWO, PAGES 21–3: WAITING FOR THE FIRST GHOST

SUMMARY

- Scrooge wakes up and the bell of the church clock rings twelve times even though Scrooge went to bed after 2 a.m.
- He looks out of the window – it is still very cold and foggy and there is no one to be seen.
- Scrooge listens for the bell to chime 1 a.m., the time that Marley said his first visitor would arrive.
- The first Ghost arrives just as the bell chimes.

WHY IS THIS SECTION IMPORTANT?

A We see that although Scrooge says he doesn't believe that he saw Marley's Ghost he is still **anxious** about what might happen.

B Dickens continues to use weather and sound to reflect **tension**.

C The narrator creates a sense of **anxiety**.

KEY STYLE: CREATING TENSION (A02)

We know a ghost is about to visit but Dickens makes this more dramatic by building up tension and suspense through the gloomy atmosphere and the bell ringing the time. The reminders of the cold, dark weather outside and the chiming of the bell contribute to the sinister atmosphere. The bell is in a nearby church clock, connoting God watching over Scrooge, making judgements about him. Dickens makes Scrooge systematically count the time to further build tension and make us uneasy. As 1 a.m. approaches, we, like Scrooge, wonder what will happen. Dickens tells us twice that the curtains of his bed were drawn open. He also tells us that the Ghost is as close to Scrooge as the narrator is to us, reminding us that this story was written to be read out loud to groups at Christmas and to make us feel physically close to what is happening.

CHECKPOINT 9 (A02)

Why does Dickens describe the wait in so much detail?

TOP TIP (A02)

It is important to explore Dickens's style and use of language. He likes to extend his metaphors through his writing. Go through the novella and list all the times a church, church clock or church bell is mentioned and work out what each one tells us about Scrooge's greed.

KEY CONTEXT (A03)

Four-poster beds would have been luxury items but it is likely that Scrooge owns one not for style but because the curtains round it would have kept him warm. The curtains are mentioned again later in the novella as expensive items. Dickens uses them here for drama and tension and later to show the nature of greed.

STAVE TWO, PAGES 23–5: THE GHOST OF CHRISTMAS PAST

SUMMARY

- The Ghost looks like a child and an old man at the same time.
- It is the Ghost of Scrooge's past.
- Scrooge asks the Ghost to wear its cap, which would put out its light. The Ghost doesn't want to and says this is what Scrooge has made him do for years.
- The Ghost says it is here for Scrooge's welfare and reclamation.

WHY IS THIS SECTION IMPORTANT?

A We learn about the Ghost of Scrooge's **past**.

B We can see Scrooge doesn't want to **embark on this journey**.

C The creative description helps us willingly suspend disbelief and accept this Ghost can **travel in time**.

KEY CHARACTER: THE GHOST OF CHRISTMAS PAST (A02)

The description of the Ghost is detailed and apparently contradictory; it is like a child and like an old man all at the same time. It has long white hair but its face is unwrinkled and its skin has a youthful glow to it. It is strong and muscular but also delicate. These apparent contradictions can be explained when we realise that this is the Ghost of Scrooge's past, and it therefore has the physical properties of his youth – hence the 'tenderest bloom' (p. 23) on its skin. However, Scrooge is now an old man and it is a long time since he was a child. The physical properties of the Ghost thus resemble the memories of childhood – the memories are old and perhaps dulled, but they are nevertheless made up of youthful moments. The Ghost's clothing continues this theme; it holds a branch of holly, symbolising winter, but its robe is trimmed with summer flowers.

CHECKPOINT 10 (A01)

How would you describe this Ghost?

KEY CONTEXT (A03)

The Victorians often used flowers and plants to convey meaning (they called it floriography). Many of Dickens's readers would have understood that holly refers to forgetting the past as well as being a symbol of winter.

KEY LANGUAGE: DICKENS'S USE OF LIGHT (A02)

The Ghost has a very strange 'bright clear jet of light' (p. 23) springing from its head which Scrooge can't bear; he actually asks the Ghost to put its hat on. Dickens uses Scrooge's response to the light to show us that he is uncomfortable in the presence of this being. Light is traditionally associated with purity, goodness and truth – traits often linked to the innocence of childhood. So here, Scrooge's reaction to the light coming from the Ghost might indicate that he recognises the difference between how he was as a child and his current approach to life, which Dickens has associated with darkness, cold and fog. Dickens will later use the sunny light of Christmas morning to symbolise new hope for Scrooge.

In addition, the Ghost's belt 'sparkled and glittered' (p. 23) in different places, making the shape of the Ghost difficult to pin down. Dickens creates a sense of memories always changing and being reshaped by experience, suggesting events from the past can have different significance to us through life.

> **CHECKPOINT 11** (A01)
>
> Why does Scrooge want the Ghost to put its cap on?

EXAM FOCUS: WRITING ABOUT THE TEXT

You may be asked to write about significant moments in the text. Read through this example by one student, commenting on the characterisation of the Ghost of Christmas Past:

> Dickens tells us the Ghost's voice is 'soft and gentle' (p. 24) and appears to come from a distance away; perhaps this is intended to add to the impression that the Ghost has come from the past. However, Dickens gives the Ghost a series of exclamations, suggesting that this gentle voice has power and impact.

Uses the adverb 'perhaps' to show this idea is an interpretation of the text

Starts with a clear point and short quotation

The connective adverb 'However' introduces complexity to the analysis, showing the student is linking and contrasting ideas from the text

Now you try it:

This paragraph needs to link the ideas to show how they work together to create character. Continue the paragraph and suggest why Dickens has done this and the effect he has achieved. Start: *This creates the sense that the Ghost …*

STAVE TWO, PAGES 25–30: SCROOGE'S UNHAPPY CHILDHOOD

SUMMARY

- The Ghost of Christmas Past shows Scrooge a scene from his childhood, when Scrooge had to spend Christmas at school with only books for company.
- Scrooge remembers the carol singer he chased away from the office and regrets his actions.
- They see another Christmas where Scrooge is once again left at school for Christmas. However, this time his sister, Fan, arrives to take him home after persuading their father to let him return to the family.
- The old Scrooge responds emotionally to these memories.
- We learn that Scrooge loved his sister but she is now dead. Fred is her son.

WHY IS THIS SECTION IMPORTANT?

A We learn that Scrooge had an **unhappy childhood** and was left at school when everyone else went home for Christmas.

B We see that Scrooge starts to **regret** some of his adult actions.

C Dickens tells us that Fred is Scrooge's **much loved sister's son**. This makes us start to wonder why Scrooge is so **unfriendly** towards him.

KEY SETTING: THE COUNTRYSIDE (A02)

The Ghost takes Scrooge to the countryside where he went to school. Its fields and clean air are a real contrast to the dirt and darkness we have seen in the city. Dickens presents this as an idyllic scene, away from the dirt and pollution of London where grief and greed are found everywhere.

CHECKPOINT 12 (A03)

What exactly does the contrast between the countryside and the city suggest?

KEY CONTEXT (A03)

Victorian literature often had a romanticised view of the countryside, and that is what Dickens presents here. The Industrial Revolution had created rapid change but much of the countryside remained the same and agriculture dominated life. It wasn't a romantic, beautiful life but hard work. However, Dickens uses the idealised romantic view in order to emphasise how different Scrooge's childhood was from his current life.

TOP TIP: WRITING ABOUT IMAGERY

Notice how Dickens uses personification and pathetic fallacy to create atmosphere and emphasise the contrast between the countryside and the city. Boys are having fun and their shouts and laughter echo around the fields. The narrator tells us that 'the crisp air laughed to hear it' (p. 26), suggesting that the air is so full of the sound of laughter it is itself laughing. This conveys a joyful, happy atmosphere far from the oppressive, dismal atmosphere of the city. Make sure that you can pick out key images and write about their effect.

KEY CHARACTER: SCROOGE

Scrooge's response to being shown the countryside of his childhood is immediate: his lip trembles, there is a catch in his voice, and the Ghost suggests he is crying. Dickens develops our understanding of Scrooge as he reacts emotionally to the memory of the boy left at school for Christmas. The narrator encourages us to work out that Scrooge was that boy. This makes us more involved in the story and increases our sympathy for Scrooge. The short statements, 'Scrooge said he knew it. And he sobbed' (p. 26) are bleak and moving. The lack of detail suggests that Scrooge is too upset to develop the description. His emotional state contrasts with that of the proud, mean-spirited man we met in Stave One, but

we must not forget all that we have previously learnt about him – this is just the start of the change and it is not going to be a fast process for Scrooge.

AIMING HIGH: DICKENS'S USE OF CHARACTERS

It's important to consider how Dickens uses his characters in this novella. He uses Scrooge's younger sister, Fan, to provide contrast to Scrooge. When she arrives to collect young Scrooge so that he can join the family for Christmas she is full of life and joy: she comes 'darting in' (p. 28) and is 'brimful of glee' (p. 29), suggesting abundant energy. Dickens makes this touching scene sharper by suggesting that the only reason the young Scrooge was left at school by himself over Christmas was that his father didn't want him at home.

Fan describes their home as transformed into 'Heaven' (p. 29). The idea that their father has changed from someone who sends his son away and refuses to have him in the house, to a parent who makes a home heavenly, suggests that Scrooge too can change. To top it all, the young Scrooge will not have to return to school but is 'to be a man' (p. 29), meaning that he will be apprenticed and learn a trade. Here Dickens is suggesting that Scrooge had a future to look forward to.

CHECKPOINT 13 A01

What is your response to Scrooge at this point?

KEY CONTEXT A03

Ali Baba and the Genii are characters from the *Arabian Nights* (a collection of short fairy tales). These were very popular in Victorian times and Dickens uses them as a kind of short-hand to tell his readers that the young Scrooge immersed himself in a variety of fantastical and imaginative stories. This helps to emphasise the difference between the young and the adult Scrooge.

KEY LANGUAGE: DICKENS'S USE OF HUMOUR

Before he leaves the school, the young Scrooge and his sister have a glass of poor-quality wine and some indigestible cake with the schoolmaster. This little scene is typical of Dickens – it is humorous and telling. Everything seems to be done for show – the 'best-parlour' is freezing cold and even the traditional pictures and fittings have been affected by the cold. They are offered a glass of 'curiously light wine' and a piece of 'curiously heavy cake' (p. 29). Dickens's description is amusing because cake is supposed to be light and wine is meant to have 'body' or depth to it. The use of the adverb 'curiously' implies the viewpoint of the narrator, and reminds us that it is he who is relaying the events. Use of vocabulary such as this is typical of Dickens's work.

AIMING HIGH: COMMENT ON THE PRESENTATION OF CHILDHOOD

Despite the fact that they sent children to work down mines, up chimneys and in dangerous factories, the Victorians held an idealised view of childhood as a time of innocence and purity. It is important to consider how Dickens presents this view: throughout this text the child has redemptive powers for Scrooge, starting with these images of Scrooge as a child, 'a lonely boy was reading near a feeble fire' (p. 27), and of Tiny Tim, 'Spirit of Tiny Tim, thy childish essence was from God!' (p. 78), which is the final jolt in the closing pages that Scrooge needs to reform.

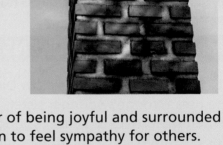

We are shown that Scrooge had an unhappy childhood, but knew love from his sister who is presented extremely positively. Dickens shows that Scrooge experienced sad, lonely times in his childhood but also happy ones. Reconnecting with these past feelings – either of being lonely and vulnerable, or of being joyful and surrounded by loved ones – enables Scrooge to begin to feel sympathy for others.

REVISION FOCUS: CHARACTERISATION OF FAN AND FRED

Make sure you understand how Dickens uses characters. The way Scrooge feels about Fan directly affects the way he regards Fred. Reread the novella and pick out the descriptions of Fan and Fred and note where they are similar.

TOP TIP (A02)

It is important to understand how Dickens presents children and childhood. Go through the novella and make a list of the children mentioned and the way that they are presented in relation to Scrooge.

STAVE TWO, PAGES 30–4: FEZZIWIG'S PARTY

SUMMARY

- We learn that Scrooge was apprenticed to a man called Fezziwig.
- We see a scene from when Scrooge was a young man: Fezziwig and his whole family throw a Christmas party.
- Everyone has a wonderful time but the Ghost asks why the people are so grateful to Fezziwig when the party cost little money.
- Scrooge defends Fezziwig and explains how much happiness he has given. He also regrets how badly he has treated Bob Cratchit.

WHY IS THIS SECTION IMPORTANT?

A We learn that the young Scrooge was full of **fun** and had **friends** and a **good employer**.

B Dickens shows that it is **people rather than money** that create happiness.

C We see Scrooge start to change as, for the first time, he feels **regret**, specifically for the way he has treated Bob Cratchit.

KEY CHARACTER: FEZZIWIG (A02)

Fezziwig is an attractive character: his voice is 'comfortable, oily, rich, fat, jovial' (p. 31), which gives a sense of plenty, even over-indulgence. This could be off-putting, but Dickens uses verbs that make him seem lively and warm. He 'laughed all over himself' (p. 30), and skips with 'wonderful agility' (p. 31).

CHECKPOINT 14 (A01)

Fezziwig provides a direct contrast with Scrooge. Why has Dickens done this?

KEY QUOTATION: SCROOGE STARTS TO CHANGE (A01)

Dickens shows us how Scrooge is changing through his response to the Ghost's provocative statement: 'A small matter … to make these silly folks so full of gratitude' (p. 33). We see Scrooge leap to Fezziwig's defence and go against all he had said to the visitors at his office, defending 'gratitude' and explaining that happiness doesn't have a monetary value.

STAVE TWO, PAGES 34–9: THE BROKEN ENGAGEMENT

SUMMARY

- The Ghost shows Scrooge himself as a young man with his fiancée, Belle.

- Young Scrooge's face already reveals his love of money.

- Belle breaks their engagement because she says Scrooge loves money more than he loves her.

- The Ghost shows Scrooge that Belle has married someone else and has a loving family and a happy life.

- Scrooge is upset by seeing this and presses the cap down on the Ghost's head to hide its light.

- He is returned to his bedroom and falls asleep.

KEY CONTEXT **A03**

In this section Dickens refers to the concept of free will, something that was widely discussed at the time he was writing. He shows how society and events from Scrooge's past have shaped him and his understanding of the world. However, he implies that humans still have free will enough to choose their own paths.

WHY IS THIS SECTION IMPORTANT?

A We learn that Scrooge had **experienced love** but **chose money**.

B Scrooge learns the implications of his earlier decisions when he believed money was essential for **happiness**.

C Scrooge shows that he still **hurts** from the loss of Belle, suggesting that he might now **regret** that decision.

CHECKPOINT 15 **A02**

Look at the description that introduces Belle. Why has Dickens made her tears sparkle?

KEY QUOTATION: SCROOGE'S CHARACTER **A01**

By the end of Stave Two, Dickens has shown us how the younger Scrooge chose money and wealth over emotional love. 'There was an eager, greedy, restless motion in the eye, which showed the passion that had taken root' (p. 34). This 'passion' is the love of money, also called avarice, which is responsible for turning Scrooge into the miserly old man we first met. Dickens's use of a list of adverbs is typical and creates a sense of the overwhelming nature of Scrooge's greed.

KEY THEME: GREED (A02)

Dickens makes it clear that greed will lead to unhappiness. Belle breaks off their engagement, saying Scrooge now loves money more than he loves her. She calls money his 'idol' (p. 35), suggesting that he not only loves it but also worships it as a false god. This Scrooge is far removed from the young boy who was apprenticed to Fezziwig and had so much energy at the party. We learn that this Scrooge has ambition to prosper and achieve success in the world, and that he once wanted to succeed for them both but now, as Belle says, the 'nobler aspirations' have gone, leaving only 'the master-passion, Gain' (p. 35). He is no longer the man she fell in love with, and, furthermore, Belle knows she is now not the sort of woman Scrooge values because she is still poor. She leaves him wishing him happiness 'in the life you have chosen' (p. 36).

In this scene Dickens sets emotional love directly against Scrooge's love of money. Belle's dignity ensures that we see she is making the better choice and once again we are invited to reject Scrooge and his poor choices; Dickens suggests that financial wealth will lead Scrooge to poverty of love and emotion. Indeed, this is exactly what we are shown in the final scene (in which Dickens 'cheats' because this isn't from Scrooge's memories but is presented to show him what he gave up when he chose money.) Belle has a loving family and husband whereas Scrooge is 'quite alone in the world' (p. 38). The contrast is effective and Dickens has made his point clear: love of money can destroy human love.

> **CHECKPOINT 16** (A02)
>
> In what different ways does Dickens show happiness not linked to money in Stave Two?

REVISION FOCUS: FOCUS ON MEMORIES

Make sure that you know the significance of each memory. Scrooge has experienced lots of memories in this Stave and you need to remember them and what they signify. Create a timeline to show which event happened at which stage of Scrooge's life. Against each event note the lessons Scrooge learned from it and the most important quotation related to it.

STAVE THREE, PAGES 40–7: THE GHOST OF CHRISTMAS PRESENT AND CHRISTMAS IN THE CITY

SUMMARY

- Scrooge wakes before 1 a.m. and fearfully waits for the next Ghost.
- The Ghost of Christmas Present appears in the next room, surrounded by Christmas food and holding a torch of fire.
- They visit scenes around the City where the weather is bad, but people are full of joy.
- There is a sense of excess and celebration in the wealthy part of the City.
- People who can't afford their own ovens take their Christmas meals to be cooked at the baker and the Ghost sprinkles incense on these people and their food.
- Scrooge questions the reason for closing everything on Sundays.

WHY IS THIS SECTION IMPORTANT?

A We see Scrooge hasn't yet learned the need to **change**.

B Dickens portrays a sense of **joy** in regard to Christmas, but hints at **inequality** in society.

KEY CHARACTER: SCROOGE

Dickens makes Scrooge's true feelings very clear when the bell strikes one and he is 'taken with a violent fit of trembling' (p. 41). This reaction shows Scrooge's fear, but it is important to see that he is also fighting the suggestions the Ghosts have made. The final change in Scrooge has to be a real and permanent one. At this stage he has not yet seen enough for a permanent transformation to take place.

Scrooge's determination not to be afraid or surprised has gone. He enters the scene 'timidly' and looks at the Ghost 'reverently' (p. 42). These adverbs make us sorry for Scrooge and show that he does have the ability to be humble. However, Dickens makes Scrooge respond uncharitably to the Ghost's mention of 'More than eighteen hundred' brothers (p. 43) in order to show us that Scrooge hasn't actually reformed: he knows the Ghost will take him on a journey but he just wants it to be over and done with.

STAVE THREE, PAGES 47–53: CHRISTMAS AT THE CRATCHITS

SUMMARY

- The Ghost takes Scrooge to the Cratchits' home where they have made an effort to make Christmas special.
- The family enjoy their meal even though it isn't enough for them.
- The family raise a toast to honour Scrooge as the employer whose money has paid for their Christmas feast. Mrs Cratchit finds this difficult and it is clear she doesn't like or respect Scrooge.
- Scrooge is told that Tiny Tim will die if the future doesn't change.

WHY IS THIS SECTION IMPORTANT?

A Dickens presents the Cratchits as the **face of the poor**, thus making it easier to empathise with their situation.

B The **joy** with which the family deal with their situation emphasises Scrooge's **unreasonable** view of the poor.

C It is the first time that Scrooge feels **guilt** and **concern** for others as he considers Tiny Tim's doubtful future.

KEY SETTING: THE CRATCHITS' HOUSE (A02)

The Cratchits' 'four-roomed house' (p. 47) is based on the house Dickens lived in as a child. Like many of the poor they have an open fire, but no oven, so they have taken their goose to be cooked at the baker's. The narrator gently mocks their enthusiasm: they cannot distinguish the smell of their goose from all the others cooking alongside it. However, our impression of them is favourable due to the overwhelming sense of energy and excitement conveyed in this joyful scene; the children 'danced about the table' and even the potatoes are personified as knocking on the lid of the saucepan 'to be let out and peeled' (p. 48). Dickens invites us to compare this home with Scrooge's cold and lonely house.

KEY CONTEXT (A03)

Tiny Tim can be a challenging character for modern readers due to the way Dickens presents his disability as something to be pitied, implying he cannot contribute to society. However, for Victorian readers, this was the norm: an individual's value to society was directly linked to what they contributed physically.

CHECKPOINT 18 (A02)

How does this scene contrast with Scrooge's lifestyle?

KEY CONTEXT **A03**

According to Peter Ackroyd's biography of Dickens (1990) it is estimated that in 1839 almost half of all funerals in London were for children younger than ten years old. Victorian audiences would have understood that Tiny Tim's early death was highly likely.

CHECKPOINT 19 **A01**

Why does Dickens make Mrs Cratchit object to Bob's toast to Scrooge?

TOP TIP **A01**

It is important to understand how Dickens uses food and drink to bring this scene to life. List all the food and drink mentioned along with the verbs and figurative language used to describe each item.

KEY CHARACTERS: THE CRATCHIT FAMILY **A02**

The family is described with a sense of positive energy: they are all taking part in the preparations for Christmas, and 'two smaller Cratchits' come 'tearing in, screaming' (p. 47) about how wonderful their goose smells as it cooks.

Mrs Cratchit's gown has been mended and patched up many times but she has added ribbons, which are cheap, to make it seem better. She and her daughter are described as being 'brave' (p. 47) in these ribbons, showing us that they know they are not well dressed, but are making the most of their situation.

The sense of fun in the family is extended as they hear their father, Bob Cratchit, returning from church with Tiny Tim. Martha, one of the daughters, hides and Mrs Cratchit joins in with the joke, pretending to Bob that Martha is not able to join them. This incident gives us a real sense of the close family unit that Dickens is promoting, and that Scrooge is lacking. There is laughter and joy, and, despite their social position and financial situation, there is happiness.

Even though the family treat their Christmas meal as a feast it is clear to us that it is no such thing. It is 'eked out' (p. 50), meaning made to go further, by the stuffing, potatoes and apple sauce, all cheap ingredients. When the tiny pudding is also brought out Dickens describes how the family praise it and do not acknowledge how small it is, demonstrating the Cratchits' sense of pride that they are surviving and achieving despite their low social situation.

Finally, the Cratchits sit around the fire and Bob proposes a toast to Scrooge, as 'Founder of the Feast' (p. 52) – after all it is the money Scrooge pays Bob as wages that has paid for their meal. Mrs Cratchit is not nearly as charitable as Bob and has to be reminded not to say what she thinks of her husband's employer because the children are present. Her function is to ensure that the reader knows the **irony** of toasting Scrooge when the Cratchits have such a small feast.

KEY QUOTATION: BOB'S CHARACTER **A01**

Dickens presents Bob as a gentle father, especially when he speaks of Tiny Tim, for example, 'Bob's voice was tremulous when he told them this, and trembled more when he said that Tiny Tim was growing strong and hearty' (p. 49). Dickens links the **adjective** 'tremulous' and **verb** 'trembled' by **alliteration** to emphasise the frailty in Bob's voice – a frailty that tells us he knows his son's future is not certain and he is not growing in strength and health as he claims.

KEY CONTEXT: THE DISABLED CHILD (A03)

The physically disabled saintly child is a stock character from Victorian literature. Essentially, Dickens uses Tim to provoke sympathy and elicit support for his social message – he is the embodiment of the 'surplus population' (p. 8) Scrooge dismissed in Stave One. However difficult a modern reader might find this use of a disabled character, it must be remembered that Victorian England was a very different place, where such characters had no independent means. The economy valued those who were able to contribute physically, especially with the move from agriculture to industrial manufacture. Dickens finds a 'use' for such people – to encourage charitable giving and support his moral message.

The narrator comments on Tiny Tim's inability to walk unaided, before describing his personality, focusing on the 'little crutch' and 'iron frame' (p. 48), which, Dickens suggests, entrap as much as they support. This is a metaphor for the fact that the poor in Victorian England could only survive day-to-day by working in low-paid positions such as Bob Cratchit's job with Scrooge, which allowed them to maintain their standard of living, but never improve it. Here Dickens wants his readers to reflect on the inequality in society as well as on the character of Tiny Tim.

The Ghost reminds Scrooge of his earlier words to shame him into realising the role he has played in the Cratchits' poverty: 'If he be like to die, he had better do it, and decrease the surplus population' (p. 52). Notice how Dickens develops his political comment, making the Ghost question the power that some people have assumed to 'decide what men shall live, what men shall die' (p. 52). This strong speech affects Scrooge greatly, and is also a comment on the Malthusian theories Dickens so strongly opposed.

> **CHECKPOINT 20 (A02)**
>
> Do you believe that Scrooge really cares about Tiny Tim? Write down all the evidence in the text that he might be starting to change.

EXAM FOCUS: WRITING ABOUT THE CRATCHITS (A02)

You may be asked to write about how Dickens presents the Cratchits so that we admire them and their attitude to life. Read this example which comments on their function:

> The simple enthusiasm and joy with which the Cratchits celebrate Christmas and spending time with each other provides a direct contrast to Scrooge. They 'laughed tremendously at the idea of Peter's being a man of business' (p. 53) which is due to his young age but it also emphasises there is more to life than that route Scrooge chose. Martha describes her tiring work but doesn't resent or moan about it. Here Dickens wants us to see the working classes don't resent working hard as Scrooge suggested was the case when he spoke to the charity collectors.

Shows reading below the surface level

Starts with a clear statement that shows the function of the Cratchit family at this point

Clear focus on how Dickens uses the character

Now you try it:

This paragraph could be improved by further comment on Peter's response to the idea of going out to work, and what this conveys. Start: *Peter's response to the idea of going out to work is …*

STAVE THREE, PAGES 54–62: CHRISTMAS AROUND THE COUNTRY AND AT FRED'S

SUMMARY

- The Ghost takes Scrooge to see a wide variety of people and places where Christmas is celebrated.
- The tour ends at Fred's house: he and his family are having fun at Christmas.
- They discuss Scrooge, and decide the only person he harms by being so mean is himself.
- Scrooge joins in with the games they play although they cannot see or hear him.

TOP TIP **A01**

It is vital to be clear about all the different Christmas scenes that are visited in this Stave. List them, noting the venue, type of people and how they behave.

WHY IS THIS SECTION IMPORTANT?

A Dickens emphasises the **inclusive** nature of Christmas, showing it is a time for increased kindness and spending time with or thinking about others.

B Fred is shown to be **Scrooge's opposite** and always sees the best in people and situations.

C We see a different side to Scrooge as he enjoys himself, joining in with the games and having fun. He begs to stay longer, suggesting he is **continuing to change**.

KEY STRUCTURE: THE USE OF PARALLEL SCENES

Dickens shows us another happy family at Christmas, but this time without worry about money and illness. As we read about Fred's family Christmas, Dickens intends us to compare it with the Cratchits' Christmas and consider the inequality and injustice.

Fred behaves as he did when we first met him in Scrooge's office: he is cheerful and merry and refuses to be negative about anything or anyone. The scene is full of laughter, and is very attractive because of its **juxtaposition** with the preceding Christmas celebrations we have seen. Fred recounts his meeting with Scrooge but decides 'his offences carry their own punishment' (p. 57). This scene acts as a counter or balance to Christmas with the Cratchits: there we were shown why we should help others, now we are shown how compassion and generosity will also benefit the giver.

In a parallel to the Cratchits' Christmas celebrations, the group drink a toast to Scrooge, this time reasoning that he has given them cause for laughter. Fred reminds us that Scrooge wouldn't accept his Christmas wishes earlier, but he gives them anyway, showing that such thoughts don't cost anything. Dickens's structure here encourages us to compare these characters and situations without him having to spell it out, a technique that allows the action to move faster and engages the reader.

STAVE THREE, PAGES 63–4: THE CHILDREN OF HUMANKIND – IGNORANCE AND WANT

SUMMARY

- The Ghost shows Scrooge two children called Ignorance and Want. He claims they have been created by the society in which Scrooge lives.
- The Ghost says both are bad, but Ignorance is more dangerous than Want.
- At the end of the Stave the Ghost disappears and the next visitor appears.

WHY IS THIS SECTION IMPORTANT?

A Dickens uses these two children to convey his passionate belief in the **power of education**.

B They **appal** Scrooge and are intended to **shock** and appal us as well.

C The Ghost uses Scrooge's words against him to emphasise his **responsibility** for such a situation.

KEY THEME: THE POWER OF EDUCATION (A02)

The children Ignorance and Want are so malnourished that they look near death. Their 'stale and shrivelled' (p. 63) condition brings to mind a piece of bread or fruit with all its goodness withered away. Dickens's disturbing description likens the children to clawed 'devils' instead of 'angels' (p. 63). The contrast from the jovial atmosphere of Christmas cheer we have seen in the rest of this Stave is particularly forceful and makes us take notice.

The Ghost tells Scrooge that these children are the creation of 'Man' (p. 63), using 'Man' to refer to men and women, or society. Dickens's message broadens here: it is not just Scrooge the Ghost is addressing but humankind in general, including ourselves. We are told to 'beware of … both' (p. 63) these children, but especially to beware of 'Ignorance'. This might seem the wrong way round at first, for surely 'Want', or need, must be addressed; if people are without food and shelter they cannot survive. However, here Dickens is promoting education and its role in eradicating Want through knowledge.

REVISION FOCUS: USING QUOTATIONS

It's important that you are able to recall key quotations for each significant character, because that will allow you to write about Dickens's style and language. Decide on one short quotation per main character for this Stave, write it down and underline the key words. You might like to make this into a poster for revision.

KEY CONTEXT (A03)

Dickens believed that only through education could the cycle of poverty be broken. Through allowing poor people better access to well-paid jobs and by giving them the confidence and knowledge to progress in life, Dickens believed that education was the route out of poverty, crime and despair and persuaded his friend, the wealthy Angela Burdett-Coutts, to provide financial support for Ragged Schools.

STAVE FOUR, PAGES 65–75: A MAN HAS DIED

SUMMARY

- The Ghost of Christmas Yet to Come appears. It does not speak, but points the way, showing Scrooge scenes from the future.
- Business people in the City discuss a colleague who has died; they don't care about his death.
- Thieves meet to sell items they have stolen from the dead man.
- The Ghost tries to make Scrooge look at the face of the dead man but Scrooge says he can't.
- A young couple are given hope that they will have longer to repay a loan because this man has died.

WHY IS THIS SECTION IMPORTANT?

A Dickens creates a **horrifying scene** where we see the results of living **without care** for others.

B We see Scrooge is **shocked** but hasn't fully changed; he can't look at the face of the dead man.

C The **relief** of the young couple shows the **misery** that debt can bring.

KEY CHARACTER: SCROOGE (A02)

CHECKPOINT 21 (A01)

Scrooge claims he has changed so why does he still have to follow this Ghost?

We see a partially changed Scrooge even before he is exposed to the sights the Ghost has in store for him. Scrooge is nervous and can hardly stand. He finds it very unnerving that the Ghost can look at him but he can't see the Ghost's face. However, he understands that he needs to learn the lessons he is about to receive. This is a very different character from the one we first met; he has already resolved to 'live to be another man from what I was' (p. 66) and we question the purpose of what this Ghost is about to show him.

KEY CHARACTER: THE LAST OF THE SPIRITS (A02)

This last Ghost is more sinister than the previous ones. It is described as a 'Phantom', and the use of three adverbs to clarify its arrival slows the pace and establishes a graver, more solemn tone: it 'slowly, gravely, silently approached' (p. 65). The Ghost does not wear the festive robe its two predecessors did but is 'shrouded' (p. 65) in black, thus alluding to death by calling to mind visions of the 'Grim Reaper'. It is surrounded in darkness and can hardly be seen; indeed Scrooge feels its presence rather than sees it. This Ghost doesn't speak, but points the way Scrooge must go. Scrooge provides the commentary for us here, saying that we are going to see shadows of what might be if events continue as they are. Dickens changes the tone of the novella, signalling to us the serious nature of his message.

CHECKPOINT 22 (A02)

How is this Ghost different from Scrooge's previous supernatural visitors?

KEY SETTING: THE UGLY SIDE OF THE CITY (A02)

Scrooge and the Ghost go into a poorer part of the town that has a bad reputation. The adjectives are piled up to create an overwhelming sense of despair and horror: the streets are 'foul and narrow; the shops and houses wretched; the people half-naked, drunken, slipshod, ugly' (p. 69), the smells are dreadful and 'the whole quarter reeked with crime, with filth, and misery' (p. 69). Like many social reformers, Dickens believed that crime is often a result of poverty and misery. He intends us to be repulsed by the place and the people we will meet there.

CHECKPOINT 23 (A02)

Why have the people in Old Joe's shop stolen the possessions of the dead man?

KEY CHARACTERS: OLD JOE AND THE THIEVES (A02)

Dickens creates four unpleasant characters to show the depravity that greed can cause. Three people, a 'charwoman', Mrs Dilber who is a 'laundress', and an 'undertaker's man' (p. 69), enter Old Joe's dark and dirty shop to sell him items they have stolen from the dead man. Dickens brings them to life through their dialogue as they justify their actions. They claim to be taking care of themselves, as the dead man always took care of himself. They don't see that anyone has suffered from their thefts – the man died without anyone to care for him or miss him or his possessions. Although on face value these claims might seem logical, the attitudes of the people are intended to shock us because they are so harsh and uncaring.

KEY QUOTATION: THE HORROR OF A LONELY DEATH A02

Dickens uses highly emotive language to describe the corpse of the man whose belongings have been stolen and sold: 'plundered and bereft, unwatched, unwept, uncared for' (p. 73). The list of adjectives with the repeated negative prefix 'un' is one of Dickens's favourite techniques and he creates a sense of overwhelming neglect and pity.

CHECKPOINT 24 A02

How does Dickens show us that the young couple are to be pitied?

KEY THEME: THE HORROR OF DEBT A01

Dickens shocks Scrooge and the reader when the young couple demonstrate unexpected emotion at the death of the man. The husband, 'care-worn and depressed, though he was young' (p. 74), is ashamed of the natural relief he feels at the news he has heard. The dead man had lent them money but they were having difficulty in paying it back. Now the debt will be passed to another lender, giving them time to save more money. As a consequence, the news of the man's death is good for them – it saves them from financial disaster. Dickens demonstrates that this is a good-hearted couple because they are ashamed and embarrassed by their response to the man's death, but his demise nevertheless gives them hope.

AIMING HIGH: PHILOSOPHICAL QUESTIONS FROM DICKENS

An interesting area to explore is the impact that Dickens wants his work to have on his readers. From the Preface, he has made it clear he wants his readers to think about the issues he raises in this novella, and you will need to make sure you have thought them through carefully before you start to write about them. You also need to draw together important points from the whole text, not just a short extract or specific focus.

In previous Staves we have seen the risk to Tiny Tim caused by not having funds for medical care. However, the scenes in Stave Four illustrate the sentiments voiced by Marley in Stave One and Fred in Stave Three – money is only of use if you do good with it. Scrooge is a rich man who hoards his money for himself and chose money over love, but the Ghost shows him how his money will be of no use to him when he is dead.

In this Stave, Scrooge's money is shown to be a target for thieves, who justify their actions with reference to his meanness. It also becomes a point of discussion for his ex-colleagues who only want to know what had happened to it, and care nothing for Scrooge as a man at all. Dickens wants us to see the problems of debt and poverty. At the same time this novella is a warning not to make money an 'idol' (p. 35) but to use it for good and realise the truth of Marley's plea that 'Mankind was my business' (p. 18).

KEY CONTEXT A03

Dickens knew the full horror of debt, having seen his father thrown into prison as a result of his debts. As a child he had to sell the family possessions or take them to a pawnbroker. He vowed never to let himself get into that position and wouldn't stop working, even when his doctors warned him to slow down. He makes his views clear with the story of the young couple.

STAVE FOUR, PAGES 76–8: THE DEATH OF TINY TIM

SUMMARY

- The Ghost shows Scrooge a version of the future where Tiny Tim has died.
- The family are distraught and Fred has offered to help if he can.
- They all resolve to remember the goodness of Tiny Tim and take comfort from it.

WHY IS THIS SECTION IMPORTANT?

A Here we are shown **innocent** people **suffering** as the result of others' greed.

B Fred's simple **kindness** has a huge impact showing big gestures aren't required – just basic care and concern for others.

C Scrooge's change is taken a stage further as he finally **realises** that he must face up to who the dead man is.

KEY CHARACTERS: THE CRATCHIT FAMILY (A02)

This famous scene provides a stark contrast with the death we have seen already in this Stave. Tiny Tim's death is foreshadowed by the Ghost, for if things do not change, he will die. The energetic, boisterous family we joined for Christmas in the previous Stave are now 'Quiet. Very quiet' and the children are 'as still as statues' (p. 76) suggesting Tim's death has killed the joy and exuberance they displayed. Mrs Cratchit is trying not to cry, and blames the candlelight and her sewing for affecting her eyes. They are all trying to continue as normal, but it is obvious that the loss of Tiny Tim has affected them greatly. By returning to the same location, Dickens makes the change very clear.

CHECKPOINT 25 (A02)

Why is the adjective 'little' repeated when describing Tiny Tim?

KEY CHARACTER: FRED

Dickens makes Bob Cratchit tell of the 'extraordinary kindness' (p. 77) of Fred, whom he met in the street. Fred has only asked after Bob and responded to the sad news with thoughtful words of sympathy, but Bob takes this as the greatest kindness, reminding us of Dickens's message that it is just as important to look out for one another and provide emotional support as it is to give financial aid. He uses Fred's response to further contrast the negative responses to the death of the man in the previous scene, suggesting it is not just those directly connected with a death who should behave with consideration.

TOP TIP (A02)

It is important to consider different interpretations of texts. Some critics have accused this scene of being too sentimental whilst others see it as essential to the novella. Make sure you are clear about your response and have evidence to support your ideas.

KEY QUOTATION: THE FUNCTION OF TINY TIM (A02)

Tiny Tim is portrayed sentimentally throughout the novella, and Dickens frames him as an innocent angelic being with his narrative comment: 'Spirit of Tiny Tim, thy childish essence was from God!' (p. 78). The archaic 'thy' establishes this character as representing the poor innocent child rather than being a meaningful character in his own right. The religious language suggests he has a sacrificial function – he dies to make Scrooge see the error of his ways.

EXAM FOCUS: WRITING ABOUT DICKENS'S NARRATIVE VOICE

You may be asked to write about Dickens's style and his narrative voice is a good example to include. Read this example which discusses the way Dickens as narrator comments on the action in the novella:

Dickens is an intrusive narrator and directs us to interpret the action in certain ways. For example, when Bob arrives at his house in Stave Four wearing his comforter Dickens's comment 'he had need of it, poor fellow' (p. 76) emphasises Bob's sorrow at the foreshadowed death of Tiny Tim and his need for comfort from any source.

Starts with a clear statement that summarises Dickens's narrative style and its effect

Specific quotation embedded in the answer

Unpicks the meaning of the quotation

Now you try it:

This paragraph could be improved by further comment about the added description 'poor fellow' (p. 76) at the end of the quotation. Write the sentence, explaining why Dickens included this and the effect it has. Start: *The added description 'poor fellow' indicates ...*

STAVE FOUR, PAGES 78–80: SCROOGE'S GRAVESTONE

SUMMARY

- Scrooge realises that he must face the part he played in the scenes the Ghost has shown him, and asks who the dead man was.
- He sees a different man working in his office but doesn't understand the significance.
- Scrooge is shown a gravestone with his name on it and sees that he is the dead man.
- He vows to change.

WHY IS THIS SECTION IMPORTANT?

A Dickens provides a climax as Scrooge finally realises the **terrible consequences** of his behaviour and how it affects others.

B Dickens keeps the tension very high right to the end of the Stave, showing his **mastery of storytelling**.

KEY STRUCTURE: CREATING A CLIMAX AND EPIPHANY (A02)

Dickens makes sure we work out that Scrooge is the dead man long before Scrooge will admit to it. This helps to make us feel superior to Scrooge and therefore less likely to make the same errors with our life choices. It also increases the tension of the scene and allows the Stave to finish on a climax of realisation, or epiphany, for Scrooge.

Scrooge hasn't understood that the scenes shown by the Ghost of Christmas Yet to Come are what will happen if the present remains unchanged. Because he has already vowed to change he thinks he will be able to see the new, improved, Scrooge. He recognises his office and asks to look in, to 'behold what I shall be, in days to come' (p. 79). This lack of understanding means that when Scrooge realises he is the unloved and unmissed dead man the horror of it is even greater for him.

KEY CHARACTER: SCROOGE (A02)

Scrooge gets increasingly nervous and asks if the 'shadows' (p. 79) he is seeing are certain or may be changed – he is starting to guess the truth, although he is not able to articulate it yet. His shock at reading his name on the gravestone is the final jolt he needs to transform himself forever.

REVISION FOCUS: WRITING ABOUT SCROOGE'S TRANSFORMATION

It is important to be clear about the point when you believe Scrooge changes. List all the scenes where he appears in this Stave and write down three verbs to describe his response to each one. You might also like to turn this into a diagram to show his tipping point.

TOP TIP (A02)

Make sure you unpick the details Dickens has added. In this scene, notice how the churchyard is overgrown with grass and weeds, contrasting with the cared-for grave of Tiny Tim.

CHECKPOINT 26 (A01)

Why is the gravestone such a shock to Scrooge?

STAVE FIVE, PAGES 81–5: A NEW BEGINNING FOR SCROOGE

SUMMARY

- Scrooge wakes on Christmas Day and finds everything as he left it the night before. He is overwhelmed at having a chance to put things right and delights in everything he sees.
- He arranges for a prize turkey to be sent anonymously to the Cratchits.
- On his way to church he makes a large donation to charity.

WHY IS THIS SECTION IMPORTANT?

A Dickens shows Scrooge's **transformation** through his attitude and actions.

B We see him **delight** in the idea of treating others without any credit to himself.

C Dickens creates a balanced structure and makes Scrooge **put right the mistakes** he made the night before with the charity collectors.

KEY LANGUAGE: CREATING HUMOUR USING EXCLAMATIONS AND SIMILES

The atmosphere and tone of this Stave is hugely different from the preceding one, showing us the extent of Scrooge's changed character. The short exclamations that make up the narration and dialogue help to create a sense of joy and wonder and underpin Scrooge's happiness at being given a second chance. He can hardly speak because he is so excited. Humour is created in the description of him putting his clothes on inside out and upside down and by his language. Dickens uses a string of similes, 'as light as a feather … as happy as an angel … as merry as a schoolboy … as giddy as a drunken man' (p. 81); these light and airy images capture Scrooge's emotions vividly and emphasise the extent of his changed nature.

TOP TIP (A02)

It is important to note how Scrooge revels in his positive feelings whereas he would have rejected and condemned them in the first Stave.

CHECKPOINT 27 (A02)

Why does Dickens use so many exclamation marks in this section?

KEY CHARACTER: THE NEW SCROOGE (A02)

Dickens shows Scrooge's transformation by making him laugh, an action that reminds us of Fred's constant good humour, and we are told that there is more laughter to come; it is 'the father of a long, long line of brilliant laughs' (p. 82). Scrooge is such a different person that he realises he doesn't even know what day it is, indeed he feels he doesn't know anything about the world any more. For Scrooge this is the equivalent of a rebirth: 'I'm quite a baby' (p. 82), he says. This relates to the Christian concept of being born again when the path of Christ is accepted, and reminds us that the Christian religion allows all past sins to be forgiven when you repent of them and try not to repeat them. The religious significance of his statement is underlined by the bells of the church ringing, 'Clash, clash, hammer; ding, dong, bell' (p. 82).

AIMING HIGHER: SCROOGE'S TRANSFORMATION

An interesting area to explore is Dickens's control of the structure of the novella. He knows that Scrooge's transformation is rather extreme so, rather than try to create a realistic narrative, Dickens uses the structure to create balance and equilibrium: this appeals to our sense of order and helps us to accept the resolution. For example, Scrooge's good treatment of the boy whom he praises and pays to collect the turkey cancels out his poor treatment of the carol singer in Stave One. Similarly, Dickens makes him encounter one of the charity collectors he was so rude to the previous day and feel 'a pang across his heart' (p. 84). Once again this is an opportunity for Scrooge to right his wrongs, and not only does he give what might be expected for this year, but includes 'a great many back-payments' (p. 85) to make up for his mean and selfish years. To show his complete transformation, Dickens also makes him reject thanks, demonstrating that the reformed Scrooge believes that charity and care for others are his duty.

> **CHECKPOINT 28** (A02)
>
> How does the weather reflect Scrooge's transformation?

STAVE FIVE, PAGES 85–6: CHRISTMAS AT FRED'S

SUMMARY

- Scrooge goes to Fred's home and asks if he can join him for Christmas after all.
- He is welcomed and they have a wonderful Christmas together.

WHY IS THIS SECTION IMPORTANT?

A Dickens furthers his message about how we treat others by showing that **forgiveness** should be fast and not dwell on past errors.

B The guests are the same as in the previous Stave, showing us that Scrooge is **changing his future**.

C We believe in the change as we see Scrooge and all the guests **enjoy** themselves.

KEY LANGUAGE: REPETITION (A02)

Dickens wants to make sure there is no doubt that Christmas with Fred is a success and uses repetition to secure our understanding: 'Wonderful party, wonderful games, wonderful unanimity, won-der-ful happiness!' (p. 86). The repetition of 'wonderful' is amusing and adds to the atmosphere and the final split 'won-der-ful' reminds us that this is a text for reading out loud. It also allows the intrusive **narrator** to stress this positive state and show us there is no room for doubt.

CHECKPOINT 29 (A02)

Why does Dickens show that Scrooge is nervous about knocking on Fred's door?

KEY CHARACTER: FRED (A02)

Throughout the **novella** Fred functions as the model for how we should behave to one another. At the office in Stave One he is resolutely positive; at his party in Stave Three he provides a balanced judgement of Scrooge; now he welcomes his uncle into his house with joy and without recrimination, 'It is a mercy he didn't shake [Scrooge's] arm off' (p. 86).

STAVE FIVE, PAGES 86–8: HELPING THE CRATCHITS

SUMMARY

- Scrooge is at the office early on Boxing Day so that he can play a joke on Bob.
- He raises Bob's salary and offers to help Tiny Tim and the family.
- Scrooge gains a reputation for being a generous and good man.
- Tiny Tim survives.

WHY IS THIS SECTION IMPORTANT?

A We see the happy resolution of the story.

B Dickens convinces us of the total resolution as Scrooge **supports** the Cratchits and **saves** Tiny Tim's life.

C Scrooge finds that **happiness** comes from **care** for others, not money.

KEY STRUCTURE: A FULL RESOLUTION (A02)

Balancing the narrative at the opening of the novella, Dickens concludes with the narrator's summary of Scrooge as a man who is regarded as knowing 'how to keep Christmas well' (p. 88) and who never saw ghosts again. This suggests that he did not dwell on his past mistakes but embraced his new life. We are left with Tiny Tim's famous words, 'God bless Us, Every One!' (p. 88) to remind us of the Christian message of this story. Concluding with Tiny Tim's words reminds us that Scrooge saved him, as perhaps Tim unknowingly saved Scrooge, and that this small boy represents life and hope for us all.

REVISION FOCUS: WRITING ABOUT RESOLVING ISSUES IN THE NOVELLA

Dickens has carefully balanced this whole novella and made sure there are no unfinished issues at the end. Go back through Staves One and Five and note down how Scrooge puts right each of his negative interactions from Stave One in Stave Five.

CHECKPOINT 30 (A01)

Why did Dickens write this novella? What is his message?

KEY CONTEXT (A02)

Dickens forgot to tell us Tiny Tim's fate in the first draft and added it to the manuscript as it was going to the printers! This attention to detail not only stopped many tears among his readers but also shows us that he knew he had to wrap up every detail to fully resolve his story.

PROGRESS AND REVISION CHECK

SECTION ONE: CHECK YOUR KNOWLEDGE

Answer these quick questions to test your basic knowledge of *A Christmas Carol*, its characters and events:

1. Who says 'I wear the chain I forged in life' (p. 16)?

2. How many sets of visitors does Scrooge have at the office on Christmas Eve?

3. What does Scrooge say the poor should do if they don't want to go to the Union workhouses?

4. Why is Bob Cratchit cold at the office?

5. Whose face does Scrooge see in his door knocker?

6. Who says 'keep Christmas in your own way, and let me keep it in mine' (p. 5)?

7. What do the ghosts outside Scrooge's window in Stave One carry around with them?

8. Why does the young Scrooge depend on books at school?

9. How does Scrooge respond to seeing Fezziwig's party?

10. How do Scrooge's actions show Belle that she needs to break their engagement?

11. Who is 'brave in ribbons' (p. 47)?

12. Why does Bob toast Scrooge at Christmas?

13. Why does Dickens show Christmas being celebrated in so many different places?

14. Why is Ignorance more dangerous than Want?

15. How does the charwoman justify her theft of the dead Scrooge's belongings?

16. Who is 'the pleasantest-spoken gentleman you ever heard' (p. 77)?

17. What is the significance of the churchyard being overgrown with weeds?

18. Why is Bob late for work on Boxing Day?

19. Why doesn't Scrooge mind people laughing at him when he changes his ways?

20. Why does Dickens end the novella with Tiny Tim's words?

PROGRESS AND REVISION CHECK

SECTION TWO: CHECK YOUR UNDERSTANDING

Here are two tasks about the significance of particular moments in the novella. These require more thought and slightly longer responses. In each case, try to write at least three to four paragraphs.

Task 1: In Stave Four, pages 66–7, what does the conversation between the merchants tell us about the world of business and money-making? Think about:

- What it tells us about that world
- How Dickens wants us to respond to that approach to life

Task 2: In Stave Five, page 82, why is the description of the weather important? Think about:

- What Dickens tells us about the weather
- How the weather is used to convey ideas about Scrooge's change of character

PROGRESS CHECK

GOOD PROGRESS

I can:

- understand how Dickens has sequenced and revealed events. ☐
- refer to the importance of key events in the novella. ☐
- select well-chosen evidence, including key quotations, to support my ideas. ☐

EXCELLENT PROGRESS

I can:

- refer in depth to main and minor events and how they contribute to the development of the plot. ☐
- understand how Dickens has carefully ordered or revealed events for particular effects. ☐
- draw on a range of carefully selected key evidence, including quotations, to support my ideas. ☐

WHO'S WHO?

BUSINESS COLLEAGUES

FRED

CHARITY COLLECTORS

OLD JOE

MRS DILBER

JACOB MARLEY

GHOST OF CHRISTMAS YET TO COME

SCROOGE

GHOST OF CHRISTMAS PAST

WANT

IGNORANCE

FAN

TINY TIM

BELLE

BOB CRATCHIT

GHOST OF CHRISTMAS PRESENT

MR FEZZIWIG

MARLEY'S GHOST

MARLEY'S GHOST'S ROLE IN THE NOVELLA

Jacob Marley was Scrooge's business partner, and the narrator goes to some lengths to make us accept he is dead. His Ghost appears to Scrooge on Christmas Eve with a warning for Scrooge about the need to change his focus in life from money to 'mankind'.

In the story it:

- has been dead for seven years.
- visits Scrooge at home on Christmas Eve.
- is weighed down with chains and baggage that represent the concerns Marley had in life.
- is now desperate to help the poor and needy, but is unable to.
- awakens Scrooge to the seriousness of his situation.
- tells Scrooge he will have three visitors who will offer him the chance of escaping the same fate.

EXAM FOCUS: WRITING ABOUT MARLEY'S GHOST

Key point	Evidence/Further meaning
• Marley's Ghost carries the concerns Marley had in life.	• The chain it carries is made 'of cash-boxes, keys, padlocks, ledgers, deeds, and heavy purses wrought in steel' (p. 14). • These items symbolise the things Marley spent his life on – they are all related to money and protecting his possessions.
• It scares Scrooge.	• Scrooge 'felt the chilling influence of its death-cold eyes' (p. 14). • Marley's message is serious and there is nothing humorous about Marley's appearance.
• It verbalises Dickens's message.	• 'Mankind was my business' (p. 18). • It shows that caring for others is more important than making money.
• It shows Scrooge the horror of not being able to help others.	• 'The misery with them all was, clearly that they sought to interfere, for good, in human matters, and had lost the power for ever' (p. 20). • Marley's Ghost isn't the only one in this situation, clearly showing that Scrooge, and potentially Dickens's readers, can also end up in this position.

TOP TIP: TRACKING CHARACTER DEVELOPMENT A01

It is essential to track Scrooge's changing response to Marley and his Ghost. Look at his response to Marley's death, at the time of death (p. 1) and later (p. 2). He is unsettled by the image appearing in the door knocker (p. 11), and notice how Scrooge climbs the stairs. What does he do differently when he gets to his room? Why does he speak the way he does to Marley? How do you think he intends to respond to any future ghostly visitor?

EBENEZER SCROOGE

SCROOGE'S ROLE IN THE NOVELLA

One of Dickens's most famous characters, at the beginning of the novella Scrooge is presented to us as a mean and miserable man who cares only about making money. During the novella he:

- treats his office clerk, Bob Cratchit, badly, making him work in the cold and fear for his job.
- is antagonistic to his nephew who visits him at work to wish him a merry Christmas.
- tells charity collectors that poor people should die rather than be given charity.
- is visited by the ghost of his old partner, Jacob Marley, who tells him his focus on money is wrong.
- sees Christmas days from the past and begins to realise he has made bad choices.
- enjoys the present Christmas Day, especially the celebrations at the Cratchits' and Fred's houses.
- is horrified to find if he continues to behave badly no one will care about him, and Tiny Tim will die.
- changes his behaviour and supports the Cratchit family.

CHECKPOINT 31 A01

Bob doesn't believe Scrooge at first when Scrooge says he will raise Bob's salary. Why is this?

SCROOGE'S IMPORTANCE TO THE NOVELLA AS A WHOLE

As the central protagonist of the novella all the action revolves around Scrooge. Even if he isn't in a scene he is watching it and we see how it affects him. Dickens shows how each scene that Scrooge is shown by the Ghosts changes him, until his final, joyful transformation.

EXAM FOCUS: WRITING ABOUT SCROOGE

Key point	Evidence/Further meaning
• Dickens makes it very clear that Scrooge is mean both with his money and in his dealings with others.	• Scrooge is 'Hard and sharp as flint' (p. 2). • This suggests his ability to hurt others.
• He used to know how to have fun.	• At Fezziwig's party (pp. 30–4) the young Scrooge is full of energy and enthusiasm. • The old Scrooge starts to learn from this scene, showing there is hope for him.
• By the arrival of the Ghost of Christmas Present the change is clear to see.	• 'Scrooge entered timidly, and hung his head before this Spirit. He was not the dogged Scrooge he had been' (p. 42). • The **verb** 'timidly' contrasts with his confident rejection of the visitors at his office and the **narrator** clearly indicates that the change has started.
• If he continued his miserly ways he would have ended up alone.	• 'He frightened every one away from him when he was alive, to profit us when he was dead!' (p. 73). • This horrifying potential future is what faces Scrooge if he doesn't change his ways. It is presented as inevitable and benefits only the thieves, something that adds to the shock.
• His transformation is complete at the end of the novella.	• It 'was always said of him, that he knew how to keep Christmas well, if any man alive possessed the knowledge' (p. 88). • He has changed his views and actions and this can be seen every Christmas.

AIMING HIGH: EXPLORE IMAGERY

It is interesting to consider how Dickens has used **imagery** to show Scrooge's transformation. Dickens's focus on Scrooge's total change of heart at the end of the novella is spelt out for us: 'His own heart laughed: and that was quite enough for him' (p. 87). This reminds us of one of the original **similes** used to describe him at the start of the novella: 'self contained, and solitary as an oyster' (p. 2). Dickens has carefully chosen his images to show that although Scrooge might be horrible at the beginning of the novella there is potential in him for change. The oyster is in a hard, sharp and dangerous shell but contains the potential of a pearl; an image we remember with the focus on Scrooge's heart at the end. The oyster that was Scrooge did contain a pearl and that is the transformed Scrooge.

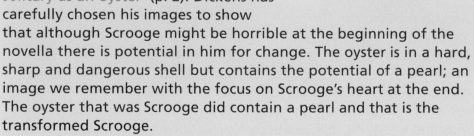

TOP TIP

Make sure you track Scrooge's change and know to what extent you believe in it. Each time he appears to respond with care or compassion make sure you ask yourself what Dickens is trying to show us.

FRED

FRED'S ROLE IN THE NOVELLA

Fred is Scrooge's nephew, the only son of Scrooge's much loved sister, Fan. He is the antithesis of Scrooge, demonstrating how we should behave towards one another. In the story he:

- visits Scrooge in his office to wish him a merry Christmas.
- holds a jolly family Christmas party where he refuses to be rude about Scrooge although he does laugh at his miserly ways.
- is kind to Bob, expressing his sorrow for the death of Tiny Tim (as portrayed by the Ghost of Christmas Yet to Come).
- welcomes Scrooge into the family Christmas without question.

EXAM FOCUS: WRITING ABOUT FRED

Key point	Evidence/Further meaning
• Fred acts as a **foil** to the hardened Scrooge.	• When we first meet him, at Scrooge's office, he stands his ground against Scrooge's mean and miserly rantings (pp. 4–6). • We can see he values love over money.
• He is the mouthpiece for Dickens's views about Christmas.	• He defines Christmas as 'a good time; a kind, forgiving, charitable, pleasant time' (p. 5). • His eloquence and confidence make him attractive and make his ideas seem logical.
• He shows us that Scrooge is to be pitied.	• 'I am sorry for him; I couldn't be angry with him if I tried. Who suffers by his ill whims? Himself, always' (p. 58). • This thoughtful approach is typical of Fred.
• He is defined by his good humour and laughter.	• 'Scrooge's nephew revelled in another laugh' (p. 58). • The **verb** 'revelled' suggests his enjoyment of laugher. It is a very positive approach to life.
• He accepts the changed Scrooge without question.	• 'Let him in! It is a mercy he didn't shake his arm off' (p. 86). • Accepting someone at face value and not questioning their changed character is very trusting. It suggests Fred always suspected there was good in Scrooge and he welcomes it.

TOP TIP: WRITING ABOUT FRED (A01)

Fred and his mother, Fan (Scrooge's sister), are the only people we see treating Scrooge with love in the novella. Look at the scene in Scrooge's past when Fan collects him from school to return home, 'I have come to bring you home, dear brother!' (p. 29). She is full of laughter, just like her son. The Ghost of Christmas Past takes this opportunity to remind Scrooge of Fred's relationship to him at this point. Look at how Scrooge responds and what this tells us about his relationship with Fred.

BOB CRATCHIT

BOB'S ROLE IN THE NOVELLA

Bob is Scrooge's clerk and represents the lower classes. He has to accept poor wages and working conditions because he has a family to support, and a badly-paid job is better than no job. In the story he:

- works in Scrooge's cold office and is too scared to put more than one coal on the fire at a time.
- represents the loving father that we see Scrooge never had.
- has fun with his family and toasts Scrooge even though he's not paid enough.
- is devoted to his son Tiny Tim.
- is alarmed when Scrooge changes and wonders if he should call the police.

EXAM FOCUS: WRITING ABOUT BOB CRATCHIT

Key point	Evidence/Further meaning
● Bob is little more than a caricature.	● Bob is described 'with the long ends of his white comforter dangling below his waist (for he boasted no great-coat)' (p. 10). ● He is a humorous figure but also shows how many people had to live without items we would regard as necessities, such as an outdoor coat.
● He is good-natured.	● He toasts Scrooge as 'the Founder of the Feast' (p. 52). ● Scrooge doesn't pay him enough but Bob still does what he considers to be the right thing even though Scrooge would never know or care.
● He doesn't try to fight life's problems.	● In the version of the future shown to us by the Ghost of Christmas Yet to Come, Bob is devastated by Tiny Tim's death but 'He was reconciled to what had happened' (p. 77). ● This reminds us that death of children was commonplace and Bob always knew he didn't have the means to protect Tim.

AIMING HIGH: COMMENT ON CHARACTER FUNCTIONS

Consider why Dickens doesn't dwell on the impact that the foreshadowed death of Tiny Tim has on Bob and his family, or indeed how the boy died. The function of these characters and this death is to demonstrate to Scrooge the greater responsibility he has for other human beings. As Bob's employer Scrooge needs to make sure he pays him a fair wage and even take an interest in his family.

TOP TIP

Think about how Bob and the Cratchit family represent the lower classes in Victorian London. Go through the novella and write down what we learn about how they live and work.

THE GHOSTS OF CHRISTMAS

These three Ghosts act as metaphors for Scrooge's life. They represent what he has been, what he is, and what he is going to be if he doesn't change.

THE GHOST OF CHRISTMAS PAST'S ROLE IN THE NOVELLA

This Ghost personifies what Scrooge has been. It takes Scrooge on a journey to see his past Christmases. In the novella it:

- appears as a strange figure – an old man and a child combined.
- takes Scrooge to see the time he was left at school for Christmas and another when his sister arrived to take him home.
- shows Scrooge the joy created by Fezziwig's party, a time when the young Scrooge was enthusiastic.
- makes Scrooge watch Belle breaking off her engagement to him as she realises he loves money more than her.
- shows Scrooge that Belle married and has led a happy family life.

TOP TIP (A02)

Make sure you track the way this Ghost treats Scrooge, in particular how it speaks to him and makes him watch certain scenes.

CHECKPOINT 32 (A01)

How many scenes does the Ghost of Christmas Past show Scrooge?

AIMING HIGH: COMMENT ON COMPLEX DESCRIPTIONS

If you want to show your understanding of the novella at a high level, it's important to discuss the complex descriptions Dickens creates. The Ghost's appearance reminds us that Scrooge's childhood is long gone; 'like a child: yet not so like a child as like an old man' (p. 23). The white tunic represents the innocence that should be part of childhood, and it is decorated with summer flowers, a reminder that this Spirit represents Scrooge's 'summer' years. Its cap, which Scrooge pushes down at the end of the Stave, represents the negative emotions, actions and ideas that Scrooge adopted during his later years, and which hide and suppress his true nature. Here is an image that personifies each of Scrooge's Christmases into one figure.

THE GHOST OF CHRISTMAS PRESENT'S ROLE IN THE NOVELLA

This Ghost's function is to show us what life is like for different people in Victorian Britain at Christmas and to compare this with Scrooge's previously declared views. During the novella it:

- appears in a room full of extravagant food and drink.
- shows Scrooge a scene of joy in London as people prepare for Christmas.
- sprinkles the poor with drops of water and articulates Dickens's opposition to keeping Sunday free of work.
- takes Scrooge to see the Cratchit family's Christmas and predicts Tiny Tim will die if everything carries on as it is.
- travels around Britain to see a variety of people celebrating Christmas.
- visits Fred's Christmas and lets Scrooge stay longer than intended.
- provides Dickens with a mouthpiece to show the importance of education, saying that ignorance is more dangerous than poverty.

AIMING HIGH: COMMENT ON LAYERS OF MEANING

It is vital to consider meaning beyond the surface level, such as the presentation of the Ghost of Christmas Present. This Ghost personifies generosity, both spiritual and material. It wears a large green robe trimmed with white fur, reminding us that there is still innocence in the world. Surrounded by plenty and sitting on a throne of food, this Ghost shows there is enough to go round in the world, contradicting the Malthusian economic view Dickens so hated. However, despite this Ghost's appearance, it conceals the harsh realities of Victorian life in the shape of the children, Ignorance and Want.

THE GHOST OF CHRISTMAS YET TO COME'S ROLE IN THE NOVELLA

This is the most mysterious of the Ghosts, reflecting the fact that the future is uncertain and depends on our present actions. It shows Scrooge what will happen if he doesn't change his ways. In the novella it:

- doesn't speak to Scrooge, but just points with its hand.
- takes Scrooge to see that his previous business colleagues don't care about his death.
- shows thieves gloating over goods they have stolen from a dead man.
- wants Scrooge to look at the face of this dead man, but Scrooge cannot.
- shows the relief felt by the couple who owed money to the dead man.
- takes Scrooge to see the Cratchits, in mourning for Tiny Tim, who has died (in this version of the future).
- makes Scrooge look at the gravestone to see that he is the dead man.

KEY QUOTATION: THE GHOST OF CHRISTMAS YET TO COME

The Ghost of Christmas Yet to Come personifies death which is inevitable for all humans (as mentioned by Fred in Stave One). It is a terrifying figure, 'shrouded in a deep black garment, which concealed its head, its face, its form' (p. 65), reminding us of the Grim Reaper archetype. We are unable to distinguish its features, reminding us that the exact details are unknown until it strikes. Just as time will not stop for anyone, so the Ghost will not wait for Scrooge; it just leads him from scene to scene, pointing out what he must see.

REVISION FOCUS: KNOW THE KEY CHARACTERS

It is important that you can write about all the major characters. Write down three to five adjectives and key quotations for each one. You might like to find images of them from the internet, print these off and write your ideas around these to help you remember them.

TOP TIP `A02`

Make sure you can explain how Dickens has used the description of the room (pp. 41–3) to add to our understanding of this character. Look again at all the items that surround it. Read the description of the Ghost's appearance – can you draw it? Why has Dickens made this so specific?

TOP TIP `A02`

Make sure you know the key quotations that describe the appearance and action of this Ghost. Look at the verbs Dickens uses to describe its movements – write them all down and look for the way they are linked.

PROGRESS AND REVISION CHECK

SECTION ONE: CHECK YOUR KNOWLEDGE

Answer these quick questions to test your basic knowledge of the novella's characters:

1. Who 'was not a man to be frightened by echoes' (p. 11)?
2. What does Marley's Ghost have round its head and chin?
3. What does Bob Cratchit do on his way home from the office?
4. Scrooge's health is drunk twice – who by?
5. How does the appearance of the Ghost of Christmas Yet to Come help to create its character?
6. Who objects to drinking Scrooge's health?
7. Who throws a Christmas party for his own and other people's employees?
8. What keeps the child Scrooge company when he is left at school over Christmas?
9. What does the Ghost of Christmas Present do for the poor of London?
10. Who buys the items stolen from the dead Scrooge?

SECTION TWO: CHECK YOUR UNDERSTANDING

Here is a task about the character of Fred. This requires more thought and a slightly longer response. Try to write at least three to four paragraphs.

Task: Look at the description of Fred in Stave One, page 4. In what ways is this description significant? Think about:

- What Dickens tells us about Fred's character and place in the novella
- How Dickens contrasts Fred with Scrooge

PROGRESS CHECK

GOOD PROGRESS

I can:

- explain the significance of the main characters in how the action develops. ☐
- refer to how they are described by Dickens and how this affects the way we see them. ☐

EXCELLENT PROGRESS

I can:

- analyse in detail how Dickens has shaped and developed characters over the course of the novella. ☐
- infer key ideas, themes and issues from the ways characters and relationships are presented by Dickens. ☐

PART FOUR: THEMES, CONTEXTS AND SETTINGS

THEMES

CHANGE

Dickens creates a powerful positive message in this novella – everyone can change:

- By emphasising Scrooge's initial extreme attitudes and rejection of anything that does not make him money, 'What's Christmas to you but a time … for finding yourself a year older, and not an hour richer' (p. 4), he shows there is hope for all of us.

Remember, Dickens tells us in the Preface that he wants us to accept his message and change our own attitudes as well.

RESPONSIBILITY

Dickens felt that every individual had a responsibility for those around him or her:

- Fred describes Christmas as a time when men and women 'think of people below them as if they really were fellow-passengers to the grave, and not another race of creatures bound on other journeys' (p. 5).
- Marley's Ghost tells us, 'Mankind was my business' (p. 18).
- Scrooge learns to take responsibility for the poor, and in doing so redeems himself, 'as good a man, as the good old city knew' (p. 87).

Dickens had very little faith in, or respect for, political or church movements to counter poverty. He saw the New Poor Law as harsh and unfeeling and he felt the church schools set up to help children were more concerned with preaching than helping children out of poverty:

- Scrooge shows us the difference a wealthy individual can make, but Dickens also shows us that Fezziwig's small contribution, 'The happiness he gives, is quite as great as if it cost a fortune' (p. 34), can make a significant difference to the lives of individuals.

THEME TRACKER **A01**

Responsibility

- Stave One, p. 18: Marley's Ghost explains its new understanding of responsibility.
- Stave Two, p. 51: Tiny Tim will die if Scrooge doesn't change.
- Stave Two, p. 63: The Ghost of Christmas Present warns us about the dangers of the children, Ignorance and Want.

KEY QUOTATION: RESPONSIBILITY FOR OTHERS **A01**

Dickens makes Marley's Ghost succinctly convey the whole message of the novella when he cries, 'Mankind was my business' (p. 18). This change of focus jolts us as well as Scrooge because we learn that the proper 'business' of life is not about seeking financial reward but having concern for others.

KEY CONTEXT **A03**

When Dickens moved to London as a child he was surprised and upset not to be sent to school. He later said, 'What would I have given, if I had had anything to give, to have been sent back to any other school, to have been taught anything, anywhere!' This helps us understand his emphasis on the danger of Ignorance compared with Want.

THEME TRACKER **A01**

Poverty

- Stave One, p. 7: The charity collectors explain the desperation of the poor.
- Stave Two, p. 35: The younger Scrooge tells Belle why he thinks it is wise to get money.
- Stave Three, p. 63: Scrooge is appalled at the appearance of the children, Ignorance and Want.

EDUCATION

Dickens emphasises the value of education through his presentation of the two children, Ignorance and Want:

- They are horrific in their appearance, 'Yellow, meagre, ragged, scowling, wolfish' (p. 63).
- They serve to illustrate Dickens's belief in the power of and need for education. We are told to 'beware' Ignorance for he is 'Doom' (p. 63).

We might be shocked that Dickens regards ignorance as more dangerous than poverty but his chilling, emotive language shows us how seriously he takes this issue. He does not shy away from presenting the most graphic effects of ignorance and deprivation – and makes us think about the role of education in the fight against poverty.

POVERTY

The Cratchits are regarded as Dickens's face of the poor in this novella:

- They are living on the edge as Bob Cratchit can only just afford all the family's needs.
- Mrs Cratchit's ribbons might be a luxury but they are also a symbol of her desperation to make her dress look new and respectable. She is 'brave in ribbons' (p. 47).
- However, she can afford these ribbons and the family does have a Christmas goose, 'the rarest of all birds; a feathered phenomenon' (p. 49).
- The Cratchits are full at the end of their meal, although we have to wonder if this is because they don't have enough to eat the rest of the year; 'nobody said or thought it was at all a small pudding for a large family. It would have been flat heresy to do so. Any Cratchit would have blushed to hint at such a thing' (p. 51).

Dickens shows us glimpses of poverty even deeper than that of the Cratchits:

- The charity collectors tell us, 'Many thousands are in want of common necessaries' (p. 7).
- Many of the poor 'would rather die' (p. 8) than go to the Union workhouses or the Treadmill.
- Marley's Ghost shows us 'a wretched woman with an infant … upon a door-step' (p. 20).
- Dickens places Old Joe's shop in a part of the city which 'reeked with crime, with filth, and misery' (p. 69). With this scene he shows the corrupting nature of poverty as these thieves enjoy showing what they have stolen to sell.

EXAM FOCUS: WRITING ABOUT EFFECTS OF LANGUAGE (A02)

You may be asked to write about how the language helps to shape our understanding of a key theme. Read this example which comments on the use of Ignorance and Want:

> Dickens uses a list of horrific adjectives to describe Ignorance and Want: 'Yellow, meagre, ragged, scowling, wolfish' (p. 63). These emotive adjectives combine to create a sense of desperation and danger as the final word 'wolfish' suggests they will attack or hunt if required.

A short and carefully selected quotation

A clear point about the technique Dickens uses

Explains the effects of this technique with a clear focus on a specific word

Now you try it:

This paragraph needs a final sentence to explain how this technique helps Dickens convey his message about these themes. Add one which explains this. Start: *This shows us…*

THE SUPERNATURAL

The supernatural refers to events or beings that are beyond human or scientific explanation, such as ghosts or seeing into the future. Dickens, like many Victorian authors, enjoyed writing in this genre as it was popular and allowed stories to go beyond normal human experience:

- *A Christmas Carol* is set in an ordinary location with ordinary characters.
- Having a convincing setting means that readers are more likely to accept an event as supernatural. It also makes the supernatural seem even stranger by contrasting it with normal events.
- The reader has got to willingly suspend disbelief to accept the event as supernatural rather than try to provide a common-sense explanation.
- The narrator works hard to convince us that Scrooge's partner, Marley, is dead and have 'no doubt whatever about that' (p. 1). There can be no other explanation for his reappearance than that it is his ghost haunting Scrooge.
- Remember this theme doesn't just refer to ghosts – Dickens also makes use of the supernatural to manipulate time and allow Scrooge to travel to his past, present and future and then back again: 'Best and happiest of all, the Time before him was his own, to make amends in!' (p. 81).

KEY QUOTATION: THE POWER OF THE IMAGINATION (A01)

Dickens firmly believed in the power of the imagination, and we see it as a means of comfort and liberation for the young Scrooge, who when left at school over Christmas resorts to reading stories of fantastical characters such as Ali Baba and Robinson Crusoe. The older Scrooge's obvious delight at seeing these characters again, '"Why, it's Ali Baba!" Scrooge exclaimed in ecstasy' (p. 27), demonstrates how vibrant and powerful they must have been to the boy and how much they must have helped him get through his loneliness.

THEME TRACKER (A01)

The supernatural

- Stave One, p. 1: Dickens's narrator emphasises the fact of Marley's death.
- Stave Four, p. 65: The description of the Ghost of Christmas Yet to Come creates a sense of wonder and mystery.
- Stave Five, p. 81: Scrooge has travelled in time and space but returns for Christmas Day.

CHECKPOINT 33 (A02)

Why is Robinson Crusoe an appropriate character for the lonely young Scrooge to be reading about?

KEY CONTEXT **A03**

Dickens is credited with establishing many family traditions at Christmas because of this novella. As you read of the Christmas activities, think about which of them are still prevalent today.

THEME TRACKER **A01**

The family

- Stave Two, p. 29: The young Scrooge is rejected by his father and saved by his sister.
- Stave Three, p. 53: The Cratchits are shown as the model happy family.
- Stave Five, pp. 86–7: The transformed Scrooge enjoys being part of his own and the Cratchit family.

ISOLATION

Dickens demonstrates the need for companionship and company:

- Left to himself as a boy, Scrooge finds companionship in stories – 'a lonely boy was reading near a feeble fire' (p. 27) – but as an adult he focuses on making money at the expense of personal relationships.
- The difference between Scrooge at the beginning of the **novella** and the redeemed Scrooge is considerable, and we see that it is not just due to his helping the poor; it is as a result of his rejoining society, 'as good a man, as the good old city knew' (p. 87).
- Becoming a second father to Tiny Tim means Scrooge gets some of the love and support he has been missing or refusing.

THE FAMILY

Dickens balances Scrooge's isolation with vibrant **vignettes** that show us the positive benefits of a close and loving family life:

- The lonely young Scrooge is rescued by his sister and returns home.
- The apprentice Scrooge is part of Fezziwig's Christmas party, along with countless locals 'full of gratitude' (p. 33).
- With the party Fezziwig reaches out to anyone such as 'the boy from over the way, who was suspected of not having board enough from his master' (p. 32) and Dickens wants to show the impact small actions can have.

For a focus on the immediate family we are offered the Christmas celebrations of the Cratchits and Fred's family, both showing the need to laugh together:

- Bob's 'sudden declension in … high spirits' (p. 48) when he thinks Martha can't come home for Christmas shows us the need for families to be together at key times.
- The closeness they have here allows the Cratchits to deal with the **foreshadowed** death of Tiny Tim in Stave Four.
- Fred's Christmas includes games and music, key elements of a traditional Victorian Christmas that have continued to today for many families.

AIMING HIGH: COMMENT ON DETAILS OF FAMILY LIFE

An interesting area to explore is Dickens's presentation of Bob as the loving, caring father, 'he loved the child, and wished to keep him by his side' (p. 51), because it contrasts with the relationship Scrooge seems to have had with his father, 'Father is so much kinder than he used to be' (p. 29). Dickens doesn't ever show us Scrooge's father, he merely makes Fan refer to him and lets us work out what might have happened. This emphasises his absence from Scrooge's childhood, something Dickens himself experienced as a child, although for different reasons. Through these varied presentations of fatherhood, and then the joyful conclusion of the transformed Scrooge as 'a second father' (p. 87) to Tiny Tim, Dickens constructs an ideal for the reader, showing that the past can be overcome.

CONTEXTS

CHARLES DICKENS'S BACKGROUND

- Many events from Dickens's background are echoed in the novella. Charles Dickens was born in 1812, and had a happy childhood until his father was transferred to London for his job. Dickens was left behind with his teacher for a few months before joining the rest of the family. However, rather than being allowed to go to school, he was kept at home to work and, aged twelve, he had to earn money to help the family out, eventually having to work at a blacking factory. Times got worse as his father was put into prison for debt. Dickens had to lodge with a mean-spirited old woman, and never had enough money for food.

- Later, Dickens obtained a job as a court reporter; this allowed him to see the harsh justice system in action, and shaped his opinions about inequality in society. He wrote stories about London life, first published in 1833 under the **pseudonym** 'Boz'. He earned enough money to pay off his father's debts and move out of the family home. In 1836 he married and started to enjoy success as a writer.

- Dickens toured England and witnessed many examples of inequality, especially in the cities. His concern prompted him to write *A Christmas Carol*. The story was an instant hit and was reprinted many times; it was so popular many years later that he gave the first of many public readings in 1853 and read it on his farewell tour before his death in 1870.

DICKENS AND CHRISTMAS

- Dickens is often credited with inventing Christmas as we know it today. His descriptions of shared family meals, turkey and stuffing, games, holly and mistletoe have become key parts of the modern Christmas. Even the Ghost of Christmas Past is said to have shaped our **image** of Father Christmas. Perhaps the most important aspect Dickens has influenced is the idea of goodwill to all; remember, in Victorian England many people, including employers like Scrooge, did not do anything special for Christmas at all.

Dickens's view of social responsibility was informed by his understanding of Christian teachings. He rejected rigid interpretations of the Bible in favour of more liberal readings that focused on the New Testament. Most people attended a church service and these stories reflect a general sense of 'Christian morality' where the individual is instructed to love and look after those less fortunate than him or herself.

TOP TIP

It's important to note when Dickens makes political points about the treatment of the poor and the need for education. List the times in the novella when he does this and link it to your contextual understanding.

CHECKPOINT 34

Which Ghost shows us the two children, Ignorance and Want?

INDUSTRIAL REVOLUTION

- The Industrial Revolution is the term used to describe changes in working and living conditions that began in the 1760s. During this time Britain moved from being a country based on a rural and agricultural economy to being the world's first industrial giant. The rapid pace of change put great strain on all levels of society. Workers were needed in large numbers in the cities so there was a huge movement of people from the countryside to the new cities which grew very quickly; this meant that the housing available was often dreadful. The population of London grew from about 1 million in 1800 to 6 million in 1900.

- The Industrial Revolution was good for many people; it gave them more money and better living conditions. However, for the poor, life was difficult. Adults and children would often work for long hours in dangerous conditions and then go home to squalor, hunger and disease. Dickens shows us these difficulties throughout the **novella**: Bob's need to keep his job; Marley's Ghost showing us phantoms who wish they could help 'a wretched woman with an infant' (p. 20); the Ghost of Christmas Present helping some of the poor; the children, Ignorance and Want; and the thieves with Old Joe.

POVERTY AND EDUCATION

- Poverty and what to do about the poor were of real concern because vast slums had built up where factory workers lived, many families sharing one tap and a toilet. In order to deal with the large numbers of poor people, the government passed the New Poor Law in 1834. This meant that any able-bodied unemployed people would be supported only if they entered a workhouse, which was a deliberately harsh environment to live and work in. Families were separated and the food was basic in order to discourage the 'lazy poor' from choosing to go there.

- As you can see from this novella, Dickens disapproved of this law. His time working in the blacking factory when his family was in prison must have given him a real insight into the horrors of poverty.

- As well as highlighting the conditions of the poor, Dickens worked to provide them with relief. His friend, a wealthy woman called Angela Burdett-Coutts, provided the financial backing for many of his ideas. In the 1840s they became involved in the Ragged Schools. These schools aimed to give poor children a basic education; their name came from the ragged clothes the children wore. Dickens's belief that education was a route out of poverty can be seen in the two children, Ignorance and Want.

SETTINGS

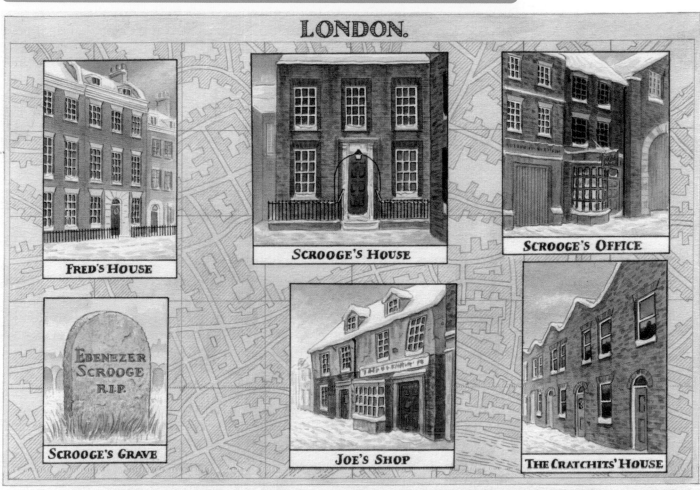

LONDON.

FRED'S HOUSE

SCROOGE'S HOUSE

SCROOGE'S OFFICE

EBENEZER SCROOGE R.I.P.

SCROOGE'S GRAVE

JOE'S SHOP

THE CRATCHITS' HOUSE

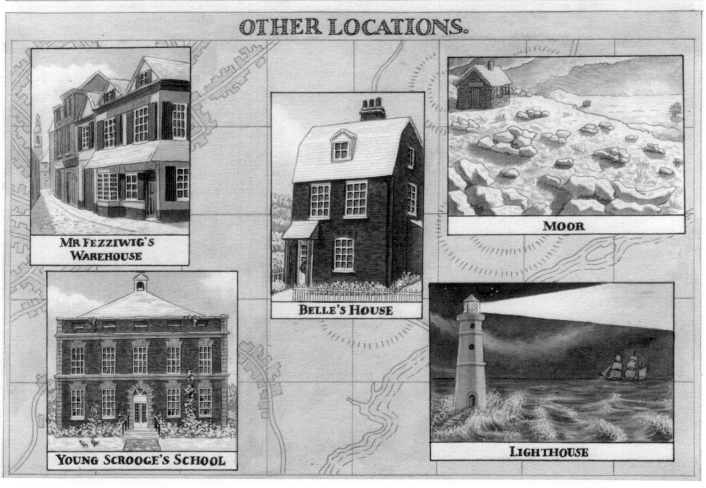

OTHER LOCATIONS.

MR FEZZIWIG'S WAREHOUSE

BELLE'S HOUSE

MOOR

YOUNG SCROOGE'S SCHOOL

LIGHTHOUSE

LONDON

Dickens uses his locations to underpin the events in the **novella**. The London we are shown at the start includes Scrooge's office and home and is 'cold [and] bleak' with so much fog that 'the houses opposite were mere phantoms' (p. 3). It is even worse in the unchanged Scrooge's future when Dickens takes us to 'an obscure part of the town' to show us the horrors of poverty through Old Joe's 'low-browed beetling shop' (p. 69). However, when Scrooge changes, so does the description of London; the fog has gone and there is 'Golden sunlight; Heavenly sky; sweet fresh air; merry bells' (p. 82).

ISOLATED PLACES

The Ghost of Christmas Present takes Scrooge to see groups of people in isolated places: miners on a moor; lighthouse keepers; and sailors out at sea. All gain comfort from companionship and music inspired by Christmas, showing that actions are more important than locations. This is similar to the young Scrooge who is left at school over Christmas – he survives thanks to companionship from the characters in the books he reads. However, his later path suggests that this is not enough for humans.

Dickens emphasises the isolation of the dead man and the graveyard. The body is 'plundered and bereft, unwatched, unwept, uncared for' (p. 73) and the graveyard 'walled in by houses; overrun by grass and weeds, the growth of vegetation's death, not life' (p. 79). These settings help Dickens to convey his message of the need to support each other and the dangers of isolating yourself.

HAPPY HOMES

Dickens shows us three happy homes, each housing a family and much laughter. Once again the characters and actions are more important than the descriptions of the places, adding to Dickens's message that what we do is more important than our location. The older Belle is at the centre of a large family full of 'joy, and gratitude, and ecstasy!' (p. 38); Bob's family are 'happy, grateful, pleased with one another, and contented with the time' (p. 53); and Fred and his guests are seen playing games that prompt 'a fresh roar of laughter' (p. 61). Dickens presents all as ideals of living.

REVISION FOCUS: MAKE SURE YOU KNOW EACH SETTING

It's important to know how Dickens uses these settings to support the action of the novella. Make a time-line showing where Scrooge is taken during the novella, and note which settings are presented as aspirational and which are used as warnings.

KEY CONTEXT (A03)

Dickens knew London extremely well. He spent hours walking its streets, exploring it when he couldn't sleep. He also walked around it with the police, learning about events and communities that were regarded as dangerous. It is thought that his description of the area where Old Joe's shop is situated came from these walks, showing his use of real life in his writing.

CHECKPOINT 35 (A02)

Dickens uses lots of triples in this novel. Can you list them?

PROGRESS AND REVISION CHECK

SECTION ONE: CHECK YOUR KNOWLEDGE

Answer these quick questions to test your basic knowledge of the themes, contexts and settings of the novella:

1. The Ghost of Christmas Past makes Scrooge defend Fezziwig after watching his party. What does Scrooge say and what does it show us?

2. What event happened to Dickens's father that changed the course of the author's life? How has this influenced the novella?

3. What links the three remote locations that the Ghost of Christmas Present shows Scrooge?

4. How does Dickens convey his belief in the power of education to relieve poverty?

5. Why does the Ghost of Christmas Past show Scrooge Belle's family and her happiness?

6. How does Marley's Ghost sum up the whole message of this novella?

7. Who function as the face of the poor?

8. Name the three happy homes that are shown in the novella.

9. What big technical and social change was happening when this novella was written?

10. What does Dickens show about people and change?

SECTION TWO: CHECK YOUR UNDERSTANDING

Here is a task about the significance of a particular setting in the novella. This requires more thought and a slightly longer response. Try to write at least three to four paragraphs.

Task: Look again at the description of Old Joe's shop (pages 69–73). How does Dickens use it to help convey his message? Think about:

- How the setting and characters are described
- How we are meant to respond to their pride in their actions

PROGRESS CHECK

GOOD PROGRESS

I can:

- explain the main themes, contexts and settings in the novella and how they contribute to the effect on the reader. ☐
- use a range of appropriate evidence to support any points I make about these elements. ☐

EXCELLENT PROGRESS

I can:

- analyse in detail the way themes are developed and presented across the novella. ☐
- refer closely to key aspects of context and setting and the implications they have for the writer's viewpoint, and the interpretation of relationships and ideas. ☐

TOP TIP (A02)

Don't be scared to use technical terms to help you explain Scrooge's change in each part of the novella.

TOP TIP (A02)

Draw a graph to show the structure of the action. Label it with the technical terms and the key events at those points.

FORM

A Christmas Carol is a **novella**, a prose **narrative** that is halfway between a short story and a **novel**. Dickens has called each section a Stave instead of a Chapter. A stave is the five lines that music is written on. This is Dickens's way of playing with the novella form and reminding us that this is a Christmas story, rather like the carols sung at Christmas time – it contains a message of new life and possibilities. Just as there are five lines in the musical stave, so there are five movements to his story. He also wrote this story to be read aloud, much as carols are sung aloud.

STRUCTURE

A Christmas Carol follows the typical structure of a novella, differing from a novel in that there is only one **reversal**, rather than several. The scene is set and characters are established very quickly. It is made clear to us that Marley is indeed dead, and the excessive focus on him makes us realise that he will be significant. This becomes true when he becomes the **precipitating incident** that sets the story in motion.

The text then follows the standard structure for a novella with each ghost developing the action, or creating **rising action**. Scrooge's repentance adds to this but he faces a reversal when he will not look at the face of the dead man in the bed. This leads to the **climax** when his gravestone is revealed: the moment of highest impact and **tension** and the one that causes the permanent change in Scrooge due to his **epiphany**. Stave Five follows the path of **falling action** as we see how Scrooge has in fact changed, leading to the **resolution** where Tiny Tim has *not* died.

AIMING HIGH: DICKENS'S USE OF STRUCTURE

It is interesting to consider how Dickens's simple structure helps convey his message. He uses Marley's Ghost to tell us what will happen, 'You will be haunted … by Three Spirits' (p. 19), and proceeds to follow that path. Along with Scrooge, after the Ghost of Christmas Past's visit, we know exactly what to expect. Setting up the structure in this way means that Dickens can concentrate on the messages he wants to convey rather than ensuring we understand the plot. He even writes to us in the Preface to tell us that the message is the important element.

LANGUAGE

OVERVIEW

- Dickens creates a first-person intrusive **narrator** to guide us through this story, making sure we notice key points and respond to characters as he wants.
- Dickens is famous for his use of language to describe people, places and features of landscape and we see this in *A Christmas Carol*.
- His time as a court reporter and his walks around London added to his ability to describe places and events with a direct realism that help him bring his stories to life.

LANGUAGE DEVICE: NARRATIVE VOICE

What is narrative voice?	The voice telling the story
Example	'Scrooge resumed his labours with an improved opinion of himself' (p. 8)
Effect	Dickens uses his narrator to ensure we know how Scrooge responds to different events, such as his 'improved opinion of himself' (p. 8) after his exchange with the charity collectors, his shock at seeing Marley's face in his door knocker, and through the words Scrooge hears when facing the dead man in the bed. These insights into Scrooge's thoughts and feelings throughout the novella make it easier for us to accept Scrooge's transformation.

Dickens creates an intrusive narrator in this novella, establishing a clear voice from the opening where the first person is used, 'Mind! I don't mean to say that I know, of my own knowledge, what there is particularly dead about a door-nail' (p. 1). Following from the Preface where Dickens has written directly to the reader about his intentions for this 'Ghostly little book' (Preface), we are led to associate the narrative voice very closely with Dickens but must remember they are not the same.

AIMING HIGH: DICKENS'S USE OF THE INTRUSIVE NARRATOR ⭐

If you want to show your high level understanding of Dickens's style, make sure you include analysis of the narrative voice. The intrusive nature of the narrator directs the reader to reject the Scrooge we meet at the start of the novella, along with all his miserly opinions. This also allows Dickens to make political comments about how the poor are treated without seeming to preach; in fact he manages to keep a sense of humour. This is established early on through the discussion of why the **simile** 'dead as a door-nail' (p. 1) is used.

TOP TIP (A02)

Look for the places where the narrator directs us to respond in a certain way to Scrooge or other characters. Write down key quotations and note what each suggests about Scrooge.

CHECKPOINT 36 (A02)

What language feature makes this a good work to read aloud?

TOP TIP (A02)

Look at the characters who aren't given names. How are they described and what does this tell us about them?

LANGUAGE DEVICE: CHARACTONYM

What is a charactonym?	A name helping to give the reader an idea of a character's personality
Example	The Cratchits
Effect	Their name links to their scratching out a living and surviving only through mutual support, acting as a crutch for each other.

Dickens makes use of many techniques to give us information about his characters. Their names are almost **onomatopoeic** in the way they help to create a sense of character. Ebenezer Scrooge, the mean miser's name, has entered our language and is used so often it's easy to forget Dickens invented it. Other characters' names are used in similar ways, from the poor Cratchits to Fezziwig whose name is jolly and energetic, just like he is, 'skipping down from the high desk, with wonderful agility' (p. 31).

TOP TIP

Look at Dickens's initial description of Scrooge on page 2. What other simile can you find there? Have a go at unpicking it to work out the connotations and deeper meaning.

LANGUAGE DEVICE: SIMILE

What is a simile?	Comparing one thing with another to suggest their qualities are similar
Example	Scrooge is described as being 'solitary as an oyster' (p. 2).
Effect	This simile suggests he is shut up, tightly closed and will not be prised open except by force. However, an oyster might contain a pearl, so it also suggests there might be good buried deep inside him, underneath the hard, brittle shell.

Dickens enjoys playing with language and he makes new similes, such as the description of Marley's face when Scrooge sees it in the knocker: it 'had a dismal light about it, like a bad lobster in a dark cellar' (p. 11). Here he describes the bacterial glow of a decomposing lobster to create the otherworldly **image** and suggest danger.

LANGUAGE DEVICE: PERSONIFICATION

What is personification?	Presenting an inanimate object or abstract concept as if it is human
Example	'The ancient tower of a church, whose gruff old bell was always peeping slily down at Scrooge … became invisible' (p. 8)
Effect	On the surface this is describing the effects of the fog, but the connotations are that Scrooge is becoming further from God and the Christian morality that is at the heart of this **novella**.

Dickens's personification of this church bell at the start of the novella helps us accept Scrooge's transformation when it rings 'out the lustiest peals he had ever heard' and makes the 'glorious, glorious' noise (p. 82) as a celebration of the new life Scrooge has begun.

LANGUAGE DEVICE: PATHETIC FALLACY

What is pathetic fallacy?	Giving human capabilities and feelings to natural objects
Example	Dickens creates humour and sets the tone when describing the Cratchits' preparations for Christmas: 'the slow potatoes bubbling up, knocked loudly at the saucepan-lid to be let out and pealed' (p. 48).
Effect	The idea that potatoes are also excited about the Christmas meal is very silly and adds to the sense of joy in the Cratchit household.

The weather is used in the whole novella to reflect Scrooge's state of mind and emotions and therefore can be seen as an extended example of pathetic fallacy. At the beginning it is 'Piercing, searching, biting cold' (p. 9), mirroring Scrooge's cold heart and miserly nature. After his transformation the bad weather has gone: 'No fog, no mist; clear, bright, jovial, stirring, cold; cold, piping for the blood to dance to' (p. 82) noise.

LANGUAGE DEVICE: SENTENCE STYLE

What is sentence style?	The range and type of sentences used, such as in terms of length or complexity
Example	Dickens uses short exclamations for the Cratchits' dialogue in the version of events when Tiny Tim has died: 'My little, little child!' (p. 77).
Effect	These short utterances help create a sense of emotion, reflecting the way people speak in times of distress and suggesting they are too upset to speak more fluently.

The joy of Fezziwig's party is conveyed through the overwhelming sense of fun and plenty provided. 'There were more dances, and there were forfeits, and more dances, and there was cake, and there was negus, and there was a great piece of Cold Roast, and there was a great piece of Cold Boiled, and there were mince-pies, and plenty of beer' (p. 32). This compound sentence builds up the sense of plenty by adding more and more in a list, implying that the narrator can only just keep up with all there is to see and do. Using the connective 'and' rather than just listing with commas helps to make it overwhelming.

REVISION FOCUS: FIND EXAMPLES OF LANGUAGE TECHNIQUES

Find another example for each of the language techniques described on pp. 65–8 and write a paragraph to explain how each helps Dickens convey his message.

TOP TIP A02

When you write about language make sure you consider layers of meaning as well as the most obvious, surface meanings. Dickens's writing often contains connotations and can be interpreted in different ways. For example, should we see the amount of food described at Fezziwig's party as generosity or selfish excess?

TOP TIP A02

Lists aren't just used for Fezziwig's party. Find another time when Dickens uses a list and work out what effect this has on the description.

LANGUAGE DEVICE: USE OF IMAGERY

What is imagery?	Creating a picture in your mind through the use of words
Example	The Ghost of Christmas Past has a long and complicated description, reflecting its complicated nature. The past is a fact yet memory is not always clear or reliable, 'like a child: yet not so like a child as like an old man' and, its 'hair … was white as if with age; and yet the face had not a wrinkle in it' (p. 23).
Effect	These seemingly contradictory statements remind us that Scrooge's childhood was a long time ago, and the child this Ghost represents is in the past. This gives us an old child, something film versions of the text have found very difficult to create, suggesting words can be more powerful at creating visual images.

Dickens creates richly descriptive scenes through his use of imagery – for example, when describing the graveyard where Scrooge's potential future gravestone lies: 'Walled in by houses; overrun by grass and weeds, the growth of vegetation's death, not life; choked up with too much burying; fat with repleted appetite' (p. 79). The exact description allows the reader to picture what this space looks like, but then goes on to touch on aspects of life and death that are not normally discussed: the death of these people has given life to these weeds. Neither Scrooge's body nor his wealth can be described as doing good after his death because they feed the grossly abundant, unwanted aspects of society, such as the thieves who steal from his body.

LANGUAGE DEVICE: ADJECTIVES

What are adjectives?	Words that modify nouns to make them more specific
Example	'The cold within him froze his *old* features, nipped his *pointed* nose, shrivelled his cheek, stiffened his gait; made his eyes *red*, his *thin* lips *blue*; and spoke out shrewdly in his *grating* voice' (p. 2).
Effect	The extended image of the cold, freezing Scrooge is made more effective by the adjectives that help us picture exactly what his nose, lips and voice are like. The fact that his nose is 'pointed' emphasises his sharp and unforgiving nature.

Dickens often creates humour through his use of adjectives, as with the description of the farewell refreshments with the young Scrooge's schoolmaster. Here the 'curiously light wine, and a block of curiously heavy cake' suggests this school was not very good and makes us laugh at the pomposity of the schoolmaster as he 'administered instalments' (p. 29) of these to the children.

TOP TIP (A02)

Make sure you have a clear understanding of what Dickens was trying to achieve through his use of these different techniques – just being able to identify them isn't enough, you have to explore their effect.

PROGRESS AND REVISION CHECK

SECTION ONE: CHECK YOUR KNOWLEDGE

Answer these quick questions to test your basic knowledge of the form, structure and language of the novella:

1. What is Dickens trying to suggest through his use of Staves instead of chapters?
2. What does Dickens tell us in order to create a secure resolution?
3. What is the impact of the intrusive narrator?
4. How does Dickens's sentence structure help create meaning?
5. How do his character names help us understand the characters?
6. What is the name of the technique where natural objects are given human capabilities and feelings?
7. What similes are used to describe Scrooge at the start of the novella?
8. What is the name of the technique that presents an inanimate object or abstract concept as if it is human?
9. What is the precipitating incident of this novella?
10. What is the name of words that are used to modify nouns to make them more specific?

SECTION TWO: CHECK YOUR UNDERSTANDING

Here is a task about the structure of the novella. This requires more thought and a slightly longer response. Try to write at least three to four paragraphs.

Task: Explore how Dickens's structure helps us accept Scrooge's transformation. Think about:

- How it leads us through aspects of Scrooge's life
- How it makes us accept Scrooge's transformation

PROGRESS CHECK

GOOD PROGRESS

I can:

- explain how the writer uses form, structure and language to develop the action, show relationships, and develop ideas. ☐
- use relevant quotations to support the points I make, and make reference to the effect of some language choices. ☐

EXCELLENT PROGRESS

I can:

- analyse in detail Dickens's use of particular forms, structures and language techniques to convey ideas, create characters, and evoke mood or setting. ☐
- select from a range of evidence, including apt quotations, to infer the effect of particular language choices, and to develop wider interpretations. ☐

UNDERSTANDING THE QUESTION

For your exam, you will be answering an extract-based question and/or a question on the whole of *A Christmas Carol*. Check with your teacher to see what sort of question you are doing. Whatever the task, questions in exams will need **decoding**. This means highlighting and understanding the key words so that the answer you write is relevant.

BREAK DOWN THE QUESTION

Pick out the **key words** or phrases. For example:

Question: Read the section in Stave One, pages 7–8, where the charity collectors visit Scrooge, from: 'At this festive season of the year ...' to 'Scrooge resumed his labours with an improved opinion of himself, and in a more facetious temper than was usual with him.'

How does Dickens **present attitudes** towards **charity and giving** in **this extract** and in the **novella as a whole**?

What does this tell you?

● Focus on **the theme of charity and giving** but also on **'attitudes'** – meaning **different characters'** views on it
● The word **'present'** tells you that you should focus on the ways Dickens reveals these attitudes.
● The phrases **'this extract'** and **'novella as a whole'** mean you need to **start** with the given **extract** and then **widen your discussion** to the rest of the novella, but sticking to the theme **in both.**

PLANNING YOUR ANSWER

It is vital that you generate ideas quickly, and plan your answer efficiently when you sit the exam. Stick to your plan and, with a watch at your side, tick off each part as you progress.

STAGE 1: GENERATE IDEAS QUICKLY

Very briefly **list your key ideas** based on the question you have **decoded.** For example:

In the extract:

● *Dickens shows us Scrooge's harsh and callous attitude to the poor*
● *Dickens presents the charity collectors as reasonable people who have thought through their actions and reasons*
● *The charity collectors realise Scrooge is beyond persuading and won't change his mind*
● *Scrooge is pleased with his opinions about charity and giving*

In the novella as a whole:

- *Marley's Ghost's contrasting opinion about giving and helping others*
- *Fred's ideas about Christmas*
- *The function of Ignorance and Want*
- *How the transformed Scrooge behaves at the end of the novella*

STAGE 2: JOT DOWN USEFUL QUOTATIONS (OR KEY EVENTS)

For example:

From the extract:

'If they would rather die … they had better do it and decrease the surplus population' (p. 8).

From the novella as a whole:

'His own heart laughed: and that was quite enough for him' (p. 87).

STAGE 3: PLAN FOR PARAGRAPHS

Use paragraphs to plan your answer. For example:

1) The **first paragraph** should **introduce** the **argument** you wish to make.

2) Then, jot down how the **following paragraphs** will **develop** this argument. Include **details, examples** and other possible points of view.

Each paragraph is likely to deal with one point at a time.

3) **Sum up** your argument in the **last paragraph**.

> **TOP TIP** (A02)
>
> When discussing Dickens's language, make sure you refer to the techniques he uses and, most importantly, the **effect** of those techniques. Don't just say, 'Dickens uses lots of adjectives here'; write, 'Dickens's use of adjectives shows/ demonstrates/ conveys precise description and helps establish his ideas.'

RESPONDING TO WRITERS' EFFECTS

The two most important assessment objectives are **AO1** and **AO2**. They are about *what* writers do (the choices they make, and the effects these create), *what* your ideas are (your analysis and interpretation), and *how* you write about them (how well you explain your ideas).

ASSESSMENT OBJECTIVE 1

What does it say?	What does it mean?	Dos and Don'ts
Read, understand and respond to texts. Students should be able to: ● Maintain a critical style and develop an informed personal response ● Use textual references, including quotations, to support and illustrate interpretations	You must: ● Use some of the literary terms you have learned (correctly!) ● Write in a professional way (not a sloppy, chatty way) ● Show you have thought for yourself ● Back up your ideas with examples, including quotations	**Don't write:** *Scrooge is a really horrible character. Dickens uses lots of horrible words to describe him. He's 'hard and sharp as flint' which makes him sound horrible.* **Do write:** *Dickens **firmly establishes** Scrooge as a miserly and harsh **character** at the start of the **novella**, encouraging us to reject him and his ways. The **simile** 'hard and sharp as flint' **suggests** his lack of human emotion and willingness to make life easier for others – something we see when he rejects the ideas presented by the charity collectors.*

IMPROVING YOUR CRITICAL STYLE

Use a variety of words and phrases to show effects. For example:

Dickens *suggests ..., conveys ..., implies ..., presents ..., demonstrates ..., signals ..., describes how ...*
I/we (as readers) *infer ..., recognise ..., understand ..., question ..., see ..., are given ...*

For example, look at these two alternative paragraphs by different students about Fred. Note the difference in the quality of expression:

Student A:

> *This sounds as if Charles Dickens is speaking!*

Dickens says that Fred is really positive when he talks about Christmas with Scrooge in Stave One. He says to Scrooge that Christmas is 'a kind, forgiving, charitable, pleasant time'.

> *Very chatty and informal*

> *It could 'mean' this, but there are other possibilities*

This means that Christmas is a time to be nice to each other and give to charity.

> *Rephrases the quotation and doesn't add to our understanding*

> *Better to use other words or phrases than 'This means'*

This means that Scrooge should be nice and give to charity.

Student B:

Fits with the idea of the overall way in which Fred is shown

Good vocabulary

Clear and precise language

Identification of technique and goes on to unpick what it does to create meaning

Dickens presents Fred in a very positive light when he speaks with Scrooge in Stave One. He demonstrates his understanding of the potential meaning of Christmas when he describes it as 'a kind, forgiving, charitable, pleasant time'. The list of adjectives implies that the good aspects of Christmas are abundant and suggests Fred is more than a match for Scrooge as Dickens makes Fred mirror Scrooge's language patterns.

ASSESSMENT OBJECTIVE 2

What does it say?	What does it mean?	Dos and don'ts
Analyse the language, form and structure used by the writer to create meanings and effects, using relevant subject terminology where appropriate.	'Analyse' = comment **in detail** on **particular aspects** of the text or language 'Language' = vocabulary, imagery, variety of sentences, dialogue/speech, etc. 'Form' = how the story is told (e.g. first-person narrative, letters, diaries, chapter by chapter) 'Structure' = the order in which events are revealed, or in which characters appear, or descriptions are presented 'create meaning' = what can we, as readers, infer from what the writer tells us. What is implied by particular descriptions, or events? 'Subject terminology' = words you should use when writing about novellas, such as character, protagonist, imagery, setting, etc.	**Don't write:** *The writing is really descriptive in this bit so I get a good picture of London.* **Do write:** *Dickens **conveys** the sense that London is full of fun and laughter despite the severe weather. The use of the **verb** 'plumping' to describe the snow being shovelled from rooftops **creates a sense** of generosity and makes it seem soft, quite unlike the harshness of the ice that represents Scrooge.*

THE THREE 'I'S

- The best analysis focuses on specific ideas, events or uses of language and thinks about what is **implied.**
- This means looking beyond the obvious and beginning to draw **inferences.** On the surface, the lists of plenty used to describe the Ghost of Christmas Present create a sense of wealth and generosity – but what deeper ideas do they signify about the meaning of Christmas, or about the way Scrooge views the world?
- From the inferences you make across the text as a whole, you can arrive at your own **interpretation** – a sense of the bigger picture, a wider evaluation of a person, relationship or idea.

USING QUOTATIONS

One of the secrets of success in writing exam essays is to use quotations **effectively.** There are five basic principles:

1. Only quote what is most useful.
2. Do not use a quotation that repeats what you have just written.
3. Put quotation marks, i.e. '...', around the quotation.
4. Write the quotation exactly as it appears in the original.
5. Use the quotation so that it fits neatly into your sentence.

EXAM FOCUS: USING QUOTATIONS   (A01)

Quotations should be used to develop the line of thought in your essay and 'zoom in' on key details, such as language choices. The example below shows a clear and effective way of doing this.

> Dickens presents Mrs Cratchit as someone who makes the most of all she has. He explains that she is 'dressed but poorly in a twice-turned gown but brave in ribbons, which are cheap and make a goodly show for sixpence'. This suggests she puts a brave face on their lack of money and does all she can to be positive, something we admire her for.

Quotation

Point

Explanation/effect

However, **high level responses** will go further. They will make an even more precise point, support it with an even more appropriate quotation, focus in on particular words and phrases and explain the effect or what is implied to make a wider point or draw inferences. Here is an example:

> Dickens presents Mrs Cratchit as an example of the hard-working poor, quite unlike those Scrooge has described, who makes the most of all she has, and so on Christmas Day is 'brave in ribbons'. The use of the adjective 'brave' implies that she is not showing her struggles but is determined to ensure her family has a happy day. It also creates a sense of her strength of character that is confirmed to us when she speaks her mind about Scrooge later in the scene.

A more precise quotation

Explanation/ implication/ effect

Precise point

Language feature

Further development/ link

SPELLING, PUNCTUATION AND GRAMMAR

SPELLING

Remember to spell correctly the **author's** name, the names of all the **characters,** and the **names of places.**

It is a good idea to list some of the key spellings you know you sometimes get wrong *before* the exam starts. Sometimes it is easy to make small errors as you write but if you have your key word list nearby you can check it.

PUNCTUATION

Remember:

Use **full stops and commas in sentences accurately to make clear** points. Don't write long, rambling sentences that don't make sense; equally, avoid using a lot of short, repetitive ones. Write in a fluent way, using linking words and phrases, and use **inverted commas** for **quotations.**

Don't write:	Do write:
Young Scrooge and his sister Fan have a good relationship they haven't seen each other for a long time this is because their father wouldn't let Scrooge go home.	*The Young Scrooge seems to have a good relationship with his sister, Fan. They connect immediately despite not seeing each other for a long time due to their father's behaviour and refusal to allow Scrooge to go home.*

GRAMMAR

When you are writing about the text, make sure you:

- Use the present tense for discussing what the writer does, e.g. *Dickens* **presents** *Marley's Ghost as full of despair and pain*, not *Dickens* **presented** *Marley's Ghost as full of despair and pain.*

- Use pronouns and references back to make your writing flow.

Don't write:	Do write:
Mrs Dilber's response to Scrooge's death was shocking, as much for the way Mrs Dilber justifies Mrs Dilber's actions and laughed about them as for how Mrs Dilber treated the dead.	*Mrs Dilber's response to Scrooge's death is shocking, as much for the way she **justifies** her actions and **laughs** about them as for how she **treats** the dead.*

TOP TIP (A04)

Remember that spelling, punctuation and grammar are worth approximately 5% of your overall marks, which could mean the difference between one grade and another.

TOP TIP

Practise your spelling of key literature terms that you might use when writing about the text, such as: *adjectives, intrusive narrator, simile, metaphor, imagery, protagonist, character, theme, symbol,* etc.

TOP TIP (A04)

Enliven your essay by varying the way your sentences begin. For example, *Scrooge becomes the model citizen, despite his attitude at the start of the novella.* Can also be written as: *Despite his attitude at the start of the novella, Scrooge becomes the model citizen.*

ANNOTATED SAMPLE ANSWERS

This section provides three sample responses, one at **mid** level, one at a **good** level and one at a **very high** level.

> **Question:** Read the extract from Stave Two, pages 34–5, from: 'For again Scrooge saw himself …' to '…"I was a boy," he said impatiently.'
>
> Write about how Dickens presents Scrooge's attitude to money here, and in the rest of the novella.
>
> Write about:
>
> ● How Dickens presents Scrooge's attitude to money in this extract
> ● How Dickens presents Scrooge's attitude to money in the novella as a whole

SAMPLE ANSWER 1

Dickens presents Scrooge's attitude to money by showing it is very important to him.

(A01) Uses the words from the question but hasn't adapted to make it flow

(A02) Reference to language

The description of his face and eyes shows us he loves money, 'the signs of care and avarice. There was an eager, greedy, restless motion in the eye, which showed the passion that had taken root, and where the shadow of the growing tree would fall.' 'Avarice' is love of money and so this shows Scrooge loves money when he is speaking with Belle.

(A01) Quotation is far too long

(A02) Doesn't tell us how the description creates this meaning

Another thing is his eye shows he is greedy and Dickens tells us his 'passion' is for money, not Belle. Belle knows this when she says 'You are changed' and 'Another idol has displaced me'. This shows us Scrooge should love the woman he was going to marry, not money and so she leaves him and he ends up being married to money. By saying money is an 'idol' it makes it seem like Scrooge worships money, like a god.

(A01) Original idea but clumsily expressed

This links to the part where all the people go to church because it is Christmas. Dickens didn't agree with people having to go to church rather than be able to earn money.

(A01) Relevant to this essay but undeveloped

The idol Scrooge worships is 'golden' this implies it is rich and attractive. It is colour symbolism.

(A02) Uses technical term without explaining how it works

A01 Long and clumsy sentence

Scrooge doesn't listen to what Belle is saying because he believes that money is really important and he justifies all he is doing and he tells her that people need money if they are going to get on in the world. He says 'There is nothing on which it is so hard as poverty'. This shows us that being poor at this time was really bad, like we see with the Cratchits and the other poor people. It shows us Scrooge is really scared of being poor and so he got obsessed with getting rich.

A01 Good to refer to other parts of the text but clumsy expression

A01 Connective to signal extension of ideas

Moreover, Scrooge thinks his attitude to money means he is wise and he is impatient with Belle for saying all this about money.

A02 Needs to explain what this shows us about Scrooge's attitude to money

A01 Sums up this part of the essay

Overall, in this extract, Scrooge's attitude to money is that it is needed and you have to have it to be happy.

A01 Style is too informal

In the rest of the novella this is pretty much the attitude he shows. When we first meet him he is really mean to Bob and will only let him have one coal on the fire which makes Bob cold. He also goes on at Fred for being in love when he doesn't have money and he refuses to give money to the charity collectors. Dickens wants us to be shocked when he says the poor should die now rather than wait if they don't want to go to the workhouse because this is what Dickens was shocked about at the time.

A01 Clearly knows the novella but races through these ideas without detail

A03 Refers to context but is undeveloped and makes little reference to the state of the poor in Victorian society

The only times we see him not caring about money are at Fezziwig's party where he is happy and at the end when he has changed. At the end other people laugh at him but he doesn't care and 'his own heart laughed' because he has learned his lesson and he knows it's better to use money to make other people happy rather than just save it all up so that there is lots of it when you die and it can't do you any good which is Dickens's message.

A01 Well chosen embedded quotation

MID LEVEL

Comment

Some good points are made here and the student knows the text well. However, the style is rather chatty and informal. The writer needs to refer more to Dickens himself and what *he* does. There also needs to be more reference to language devices or techniques.

For a Good Level:

- Use a more formal and critical vocabulary rather than chatty, informal words and phrases.
- Embed quotations into sentences so that they flow and are easy to follow.
- Include more quotations from the rest of the novella.
- Comment in detail on the effect of language choices made by Dickens.
- Link understanding to context – both social/historical and other points in the novella.

SAMPLE ANSWER 2

A01
Introduction sets up answer well

In this passage, Dickens presents Scrooge as someone who is obsessed with money, even to the point of choosing it over the woman he had proposed to. His appearance and words combine to show us this obsession.

A01
Clumsy phrasing, need to avoid repeating 'show'

Dickens shows us Scrooge's face and eyes show his love of money; his face 'had begun to wear the signs of care and avarice' and he tells us 'There was an eager, greedy, restless motion in the eye'. The use of 'avarice' and 'greedy' emphasises his love of money and 'restless' suggests he will not be satisfied with what he has.

A02
Identifies technique and uses correct terminology

Dickens also shows this love of money is 'passion' and he uses the image of the tree saying it has 'taken root' and there will be a 'shadow'. This shows us his future isn't good if he goes down this path. The idea of 'passion' links to Belle as he should feel passion for her as he was going to marry her but he didn't.

A01
Would be better to write: 'This could suggest' or similar

A01
Now needs to analyse what this tells us about his attitude to money

Dickens makes Belle stand up to Scrooge and she calls money his 'idol' suggesting he worships it and calls 'Gain' his 'master-passion'. Even though this is really strong Scrooge doesn't deny it – he justifies it instead. Dickens is showing us that this is the start of the Scrooge we see in the office on Christmas Eve.

As well as justifying his obsession with money, Scrooge dismisses how he was as a young man: '"I was a boy," he said impatiently.' This shows us how changed he is and that Belle was right to end the engagement.

A01
Summarises first part of answer and links to the question

Overall in this extract we can see without doubt that Scrooge loved money and saw that as the right thing to do. This allows Dickens to convey his message about the dangers of loving money more than people.

A01
Specific reference to aspects elsewhere in the novella

This message is also clear elsewhere. At the start of the novella, when he is in the office, Dickens establishes Scrooge's miserly nature very quickly by telling us he will only allow Cratchit one lump of coal that can't be increased for 'so surely as the clerk came in with the shovel, the master predicted that it would be necessary for them to part'.

A02
Good focus on how Dickens has constructed the novella

A01 Confusing use of pronoun!

A02 Shows the impact of Dickens's choices

A01 Losing focus on the question

This reminds us of the precarious nature of employment at the time and links to the desire the younger Scrooge had for making enough money to not be in that position. Dickens then goes on to show us that he thinks celebrating Christmas is a waste of money and time that could be spent earning money.

A03 Links to social context and the extract

Finally, Dickens really shocks us by including the scene of Scrooge and the charity collectors. In this scene Dickens shows that Scrooge loves money more than humans when he says the poor should die and 'decrease the surplus population'. Dickens wants us to be shocked and to reject Scrooge and all he stands for. Dickens uses this phrase 'surplus population' to make a political comment about policies and debates about the poor at the time, policies Dickens didn't agree with. People thought the poor were lazy but Dickens thought they needed schools and education. He shows us this again with the presentation of the children, Ignorance and Want, along with the warning to 'Beware this boy (Ignorance), for on his brow I see that written which is Doom.'

A03 Links to contextual information

GOOD LEVEL

Comment

This is a generally fluent and well-argued response. There is some close analysis of key words and phrases to convey ideas, and some evidence of contextual links. Expression is generally good, and quotations are fluently embedded, but some ideas lose focus and clarity, especially at the end of the answer.

For a High Level:

- Develop ideas about the social context more fully.
- Expand the style of expression by using a wider vocabulary so that more subtle ideas can be developed.
- When unpicking the quotations use phrases such as 'Perhaps ...' or 'This could suggest ...'.
- Vary opening sentences in paragraphs to introduce ideas in more interesting ways.

SAMPLE ANSWER 3

AO1 — Excellent opening introduction sets up importance of extract in the novella and summarises Scrooge's actions

Juxtaposing Fezziwig's party where the young Scrooge had been so happy and joyful, this scene is the tipping point at which Dickens shows us the moment Scrooge chose money over human relationships. In the 'prime of his life' Scrooge justifies his 'passion' for money, ironically to satisfy the world that he is simultaneously rejecting through this choice.

AO2 — Under-standing of Dickens's choices and constructions

AO1 — Uses short, embedded quotations

Dickens typically shows us Scrooge's character through his appearance, listing greed and 'passion' and develops this using the image of a tree which will grow to throw a 'shadow'. This conjures up thoughts of the Garden of Eden, perhaps suggesting this is the moment Scrooge steps into the wilderness and away from God, an idea that is further represented in the novella by the initial obscuring and final joyful ringing of the church bell tower.

AO1 — Develops point with reference to other examples in the novella

AO3 — Uses contextual knowledge to add layers of analysis

It is interesting that Belle uses the term 'idol' to describe Scrooge's relationship with money. Its biblical connotation of money being seen as a god would not have been lost on Victorian readers and adds a sinister layer of meaning to the noun and sums up Scrooge's absolute obsession with money, suggesting it is, at the very least, unhealthy for the soul.

Scrooge's justification of his 'pursuit of wealth' is ironic – he claims 'there is nothing on which [the world] is so hard as poverty'. Dickens's irony here is very gentle as it is only when we remember his initial description of Scrooge as liking 'to edge along the crowded paths of life' do we see his double standards in wanting social acceptance whilst rejecting 'human sympathy'.

AO2 — Specific analysis of how the technique is created

Dickens's presentation of Belle as articulate and thoughtful further emphasises Scrooge's poor choice, showing his attitude toward money has negative consequences. Scrooge dismisses his younger self: '"I was a boy," he said impatiently.' The adverb 'impatiently' contrasts with Belle's dignity and links with his 'restless motion in the eye' suggesting Scrooge's pursuit of money is a love that will never be satisfied. Indeed, the reader is led to understand that if Scrooge continues without changing only death will put a stop to its pursuit.

AO1 — Keeps the answer tightly focused on the question

AO2 — Specific analysis of language choice

AO1 — Fluent expression creates sense of personal inter-pretation

AO1 — Uses connective to shape answer

Furthermore, Scrooge describes his attitude to money as an example of him having 'grown so much wiser.'

A02

Considers Dickens's intentions and aims

A01

Useful reference back to earlier part of novella

Here Dickens really wants his readers to consider the value of money and the wisdom of allowing it to dominate. Earlier in the office Scrooge had mocked Fred for being merry at Christmas despite being 'poor enough'. However, Fred articulates Dickens's message that the emotional and social aspect of Christmas has value in itself: 'it has never put a scrap of gold or silver in my pocket, I believe (Christmas) has done me good.' We are invited to select whose 'wisdom' we follow regarding money although clearly Dickens presents Fred's approach as his recommended path!

It is perhaps when Scrooge meets with the charity collectors that the real danger of making money your 'idol' can be seen for Scrooge has totally rejected any sense of human compassion. Dickens uses the dialogue to gradually reveal Scrooge's shockingly harsh response to the poor. When he finally shows us Scrooge's Malthusian principles, that the poor should die and 'decrease the surplus population', he has made Scrooge so despicable we automatically reject this argument in favour of Dickens's far more compassionate 'ghost of an idea'. This inclusion of politics in an entertaining Christmas story suggests Dickens intends his readers to consider their attitudes to money as well.

A03

Uses contextual knowledge to add to understanding

A01

Summarises answer with reference to whole text

Scrooge's obsession with money and wealth is securely established throughout the novella so his transformation is absolute. Dickens carefully ensures Scrooge rectifies his earlier errors and changes his attitude to money: now he gains joy from giving it away and supporting others with it. He gives half-a-crown to the boy who fetches the Poulterer, thus correcting his actions to the carol singer; he gives 'a great many back payments' to the charity collector and joins Fred and his family for Christmas Day. Dickens finishes by ensuring we know this changed attitude towards money is lifelong and that it makes Scrooge richer emotionally and socially; implying, of course, that we will also be 'richer' if we adopt such a stance ourselves.

A01

Fluent concluding sentence moves from the specific to the general

VERY HIGH LEVEL

Comment

This is a convincing response showing that the student knows the whole text very well as the answer references various points from it. The embedded quotations are well chosen and demonstrate the argument and allow for alternative, personal interpretations. Literary techniques are referenced to help understand the meaning, not as an end in themselves. Expression is effortlessly fluent and the student has fully engaged with the text and the task, using a variety of sentence structures.

PRACTICE TASK

Write a full-length response to this exam-style question and then use the **Mark scheme** on page 88 to assess your own response.

TOP TIP **A01**

You can use the General skills section of the **Mark scheme** on page 88 to remind you of the key criteria you'll need to cover.

In Stave Five, pages 81–2, Scrooge wakes to his first Christmas as a changed man. Read from: '"I don't know what to do!" cried Scrooge' to 'Oh, glorious, glorious!'

In this extract, how does Dickens present Scrooge as completely transformed?

Write about:

● How Dickens presents Scrooge in this extract

● How he is presented in the rest of the novella

Remember:

● Plan quickly and efficiently by using key words from the question

● Write equally about the extract and the rest of the novella

● Focus on the techniques Dickens uses and the effect of these on the reader

● Support your ideas with relevant evidence, including quotations

FURTHER QUESTIONS

1 Read this extract from Stave Three, pages 63–4, in which the Ghost of Christmas Present shows Scrooge the children Ignorance and Want. It begins, '"Forgive me if I am not justified in what I ask," said Scrooge' and ends 'The bell struck twelve.'

Write about how Dickens uses these two children to convey his messages. Refer to the extract and to the novella as a whole.

2 Read this extract from Stave Three, pages 50–1, in which the Cratchits enjoy their Christmas dinner. It begins, 'There never was such a goose' and ends 'Any Cratchit would have blushed to hint at such a thing.'

Explore how Dickens presents the Cratchit family in this extract and elsewhere in the novella.

3 'Scrooge's change happens too fast for us to believe in it.' How far do you agree with this view? Explore at least two moments from the novella to support your ideas.

4 Explain how Dickens explores the theme of forgiveness in the novella.

Consider:

● The importance of forgiveness in the novella

● How attitudes to forgiveness are presented

LITERARY TERMS

adjective	a word that describes a noun, making it more precise
adverb	a word that describe a verb, showing how the action happens
alliteration	repetition of the same sound at the beginning of words close to each other
archetype	a universal symbol in character form intended to represent basic human behaviour
central protagonist	the main character who undertakes a quest or challenge
charactonym	a name which makes suggestions about a character's manner or appearance
climax	the most important part of a narrative and the moment of greatest emotional tension
compound sentence	a sentence made up of one or more equal clauses (parts) joined by a connective (such as 'and')
connective	a word or phrase that joins clauses, sentences or paragraphs
dialogue	a discussion or conversation, or simply the words spoken by a character
emotive	aiming to provoke an emotional response in the audience
empathise	to understand and share feelings experienced by others
epiphany	the moment of insight or understanding that changes how a character sees the world
equilibrium	when everything is balanced
falling action	a reduction of the tension in a story which allows events to slow down, coming after a climax
foil	something or someone with opposite characteristics to the subject, used to balance them out and even to draw attention to their failings
foreshadowing	a warning or indication of a future event
image/imagery	a picture in words; similes, metaphors and personification are all types of imagery
irony/ironic	saying or writing one thing but implying another
juxtaposition	putting two contrasting ideas or descriptions together to create effect
metaphor	a word or image which means one thing is used to represent another to show something interesting or different about it
narrative	a story, a series of connected events
narrator	the voice telling the story
novel	a prose fiction with a central protagonist, climax and resolution; there may be many reversals
novella	a short prose fiction longer than a short story and shorter than a novel with a central protagonist moving towards a climax and resolution; there is only one reversal
onomatopoeia	words that sound like the noise they are describing
pathetic fallacy	the presentation of objects and events in nature as having human emotions and traits
personification	an inanimate object or abstract concept is given human attributes or feelings
precipitating incident	the event or action that sets the whole plot in motion
pseudonym	a fictitious name, often used by writers
pun	a play on words
resolution	the conclusion or ending when all the plot elements are resolved
reversal	the development or change in a character is stopped or even goes backwards
rising action	the plot and action develop towards the climax
semantic field	a group of words or language linked by a theme
simile	two seemingly different things are compared to allow greater understanding of one of them; the words 'like' or 'as' are often used
suspend disbelief	put your knowledge of the real world to one side and believe in the world of the fiction
symbol/symbolise	a sign that represents something else
tension	high emotion
tone	how the narrator or a character speaks; can also be set through description
verb	a word used to describe an action
vignette	a short illustration in words, almost creating a portrait of a character or event

CHECKPOINT ANSWERS

PART TWO, PP. 10–43

1. He wants to establish his relationship with us and make sure we understand there is a moral message to this book. 2. It creates an overwhelming sense of Scrooge's horrible character. 3. Scrooge is miserable and Cratchit is full of fun and energy. 4. To emphasise how unusual Scrooge's response to Christmas is.
5. To build tension. 6. The joke is: 'there's more of gravy than the grave about you'. Dickens is showing Scrooge is fighting back so that his transformation isn't going to be easy.
7. To emphasise it is supernatural and not of this world. 8. He can't say his usual 'Humbug' and goes to bed in his clothes. 9. To build tension. 10. He is all of Scrooge's past Christmases at once so looks like a child and the old man Scrooge now is. 11. He can't bear to see the light it emits. 12. The countryside is shown as idyllic and the city as dirty and miserable. This suggests Dickens sees the countryside as preferable. 13. His emotional response is moving and we re-evaluate our ideas about him. 14. To show that employers can be generous and Scrooge didn't have to become how he is. 15. To link her with the Ghost and provide contrast with Scrooge. 16. We see family happiness when Fan takes Scrooge home and when we see the older Belle; and community happiness at Fezziwig's party. 17. Scrooge 'reverently' looks at the Ghost, showing respect. This suggests he has started to change. 18. It is full of joy and noise. 19. To remind us what a horrible and mean employer he is, paying Bob low wages and keeping him in fear for his job. 20. Scrooge's exclamation shows he is shocked and is starting to care about others. 21. His change isn't secure and he doesn't yet totally understand the dangers of his ways. 22. It is far more sinister and does not speak. 23. They are poor and live in a society where you take what you can. 24. They are embarrassed about feeling relieved about this death. 25. To emphasise his vulnerability. 26. He thought that as he'd decided to change, the future would show the consequences of the new Scrooge's actions. 27. To emphasise the joy and create a sense that Scrooge is overwhelmed with happiness. 28. It is now clear and bright, like Scrooge's new personality and future. 29. If the change is going to be worth it Scrooge has to work for his new life. 30. To persuade us to think of and look out for others.

PART THREE, PP. 46–53

31. To remind us that the old Scrooge would never have considered such an act and to show us how much Scrooge has changed. 32. Six: the village with schoolchildren travelling home; young Scrooge left at school; Fan collecting young Scrooge; Fezziwig's party; Belle and Scrooge breaking up; Belle, happy with her family.

PART FOUR, PP. 55–62

33. The main character in Daniel Defoe's novel, Robinson Crusoe was shipwrecked on a desert island and was very lonely, just like the young Scrooge must have been. 34. The Ghost of Christmas Present – this shows that Dickens saw these issues as current to him and his readers. 35. The visitors to the office; the Ghosts of Christmas; the happy homes; the isolated Christmases; the responses to Scrooge's death.

PART FIVE, PP. 64–8

36. The use of the first person ('I').

PROGRESS AND REVISION CHECK ANSWERS

PART TWO, PP. 44–5

SECTION ONE

1 Marley's Ghost.

2 Three (Fred, the charity collectors, the carol singer).

3 Die.

4 He is allowed only one piece of coal.

5 Marley's.

6 Scrooge.

7 Chains, one has an iron safe.

8 He is lonely and the characters provide company.

9 With joy.

10 He defends his focus on money and doesn't argue that they now wouldn't have become engaged.

11 Mrs Cratchit.

12 Scrooge has paid Bob's wages and therefore for their meal; Bob wants to do the right thing.

13 It emphasises that Scrooge is an outsider and makes the celebration appear the norm.

14 Lack of education means people cannot work their way out of poverty which is bad for them and society.

15 She tells everyone that if Scrooge had been nicer to people when he lived there would be people around him when he died – this would have meant she couldn't steal from the dead man.

16 Fred.

17 Whilst the grave is in a proper burial place, it is not cared for or respected at all.

18 Scrooge had sent his family a huge turkey for their Christmas meal and so he and his family had probably celebrated for longer than usual.

19 He knows the results of his actions are more important than what people think of him.

20 They provide a clear **resolution** and move the focus back to the reader. They also show us that Tiny Tim didn't die.

SECTION TWO

Task 1: Possible Plan

● The conversation is focused only on money: 'What has he done with his money?' (p. 67).

● There is no sense of care or concern that someone has died: 'I don't mind going if a lunch is provided' (p. 67).

● Dickens wants us to be shocked by their callousness: 'I must be fed, if I make one' (p. 67).

● Dickens wants us to remember Marley's Ghost's message: 'Mankind was my business' (p. 18).

Task 2: Possible Plan

● The fog has gone, so it is totally different to that of the opening Stave: 'No fog, no mist; clear, bright, jovial, stirring' (p. 82).

● The sun is shining: 'Golden sunlight; Heavenly sky; sweet fresh air' (p. 82).

● The transformation in Scrooge is reflected in the weather.

● The new Scrooge might not find the path ahead easy (it might be 'cold') but it will be more fulfilling and he will feel more alive: 'piping for the blood to dance to' (p. 82).

PART THREE, P. 54

SECTION ONE

1. Scrooge.

2. A folded handkerchief.

3. He enjoys the snow and goes down a slide twenty times with a group of boys.

4. The Cratchit family and Fred and his guests.

5. It can't really be seen clearly, just as the future can't be seen.

6. Mrs Cratchit.

7. Mr Fezziwig.

8. Books and characters such as Ali Baba and Robinson Crusoe's parrot.

9. It sprinkles their dinners with incense from its torch.

10. Old Joe.

SECTION TWO

Possible Plan:

● Fred totally changes the atmosphere of the scene with his exclamations: 'A merry Christmas, uncle! God save you!' (p. 4).

● Dickens presents him as an attractive character: 'his face was ruddy and handsome' (p. 4).

● His words mirror and balance Scrooge's, showing he is equal to Scrooge's negativity: 'You're rich enough' (p. 4).

● Dickens creates Fred as Scrooge's opposite, suggesting he will present an opposing view of the world: 'he was all in a glow' (p. 4).

PART FOUR, P. 63

SECTION ONE

1. 'He has the power to render us happy or unhappy … The happiness he gives, is quite as great as if it cost a fortune' (p. 34). This shows Scrooge is giving value to feelings, much as Fred did in the office.

2. Dickens's father was imprisoned for debt and Dickens had to work in a factory, which he hated. Dickens's political ideas about the treatment of the poor may be seen in this novella.

3. Each remote location features Christmas music.

4. He uses the children, Ignorance and Want, and tells us that Ignorance is more dangerous than Want (poverty).

5. It provides closure for the reader and allows a comparison with Scrooge's current way of life.

6. He says, 'Mankind was my business' (p. 18).

7. The Cratchits.

8. The homes of the older Belle, the Cratchits in the present and Fred.

9. The Industrial Revolution.

10. He shows that everyone can change.

SECTION TWO

Possible Plan:

● The shop is repulsive: 'iron, old rags, bottles, bones, and greasy offal, were bought' (p. 69).

● Its sordid nature isn't just made from objects, but people's lives as well: 'Secrets that few would like to scrutinise were bred and hidden in mountains of unseemly rags, masses of corrupted fat, and sepulchres of bones' (p. 69).

● The characters are repugnant: 'a woman with a heavy bundle slunk into the shop' (p. 69).

● We are meant to be shocked at their pride in their theft from a dead man: 'He frightened every one away from him when he was alive, to profit us when he was dead! Ha, ha, ha!' (p. 73).

PART FIVE, P. 69

SECTION ONE

1 He is reminding us that this is a story for Christmas and contains a tale of new life and possibilities. It was also intended to be read aloud, much as Christmas carols are sung aloud.

2 Dickens lists all the ways Scrooge changes to show he has changed in every possible way and that the transformation is permanent.

3 The intrusive **narrator** bosses us about and makes sure we interpret characters and events as Dickens wishes us to.

4 His use of lists and compound sentences creates a sense that there is so much to describe it is overwhelming.

5 Dickens uses **charactonyms** which add to our understanding of the characterisation, e.g. Scrooge is miserly.

6 **Pathetic fallacy**.

7 'Hard and sharp as flint' **and** 'solitary as an oyster'.

8 **Personification**.

9 Marley's Ghost appearing to Scrooge.

10 **Adjectives**.

SECTION TWO

Possible Plan:

● Stave One convinces us that Scrooge is an unpleasant character: 'Oh! But he was a tight-fisted hand at the grindstone, Scrooge!' (p. 2).

● We are shocked by his pride at his response to the charity collectors, the moment when he is perhaps at his most despicable: 'Scrooge resumed his labours with an improved opinion of himself' (p. 8).

● His tears at seeing his childhood location make us believe there is potential for compassion and goodness in him: 'Your lip is trembling … And what is that upon your cheek?' (p. 25).

● In Stave Four his final declaration of change is spoken in formal language that supports his determination: 'I will honour Christmas in my heart, and try to keep it all the year. I will live in the Past, the Present, and the Future. The Spirits of all Three shall strive within me' (p. 80).

MARK SCHEME

POINTS YOU COULD HAVE MADE

- Scrooge's laughter and the way it continues throughout the extract
- The similes Scrooge uses to describe himself and how they contrast with the ones the narrator used at the start of the novella
- The way he reminds us of the events that have happened

- The appearance of the church bell that Scrooge can now hear
- The description of the 'golden sunlight' and how this contrasts to the weather in Stave One
- What Scrooge means when he describes himself as 'quite a baby' and how this fits with the Christian message

GENERAL SKILLS

Make a judgement about your level based on the points you made (above) and the skills you showed.

Level	Key elements	Spelling, punctuation and grammar	Tick your level
Very high	**Very well-structured answer which gives a rounded and convincing viewpoint.** You use very detailed analysis of the writer's methods and effects on the reader, using precise references which are fluently woven into what you say. You draw inferences, consider more than one perspective or angle, including the context where relevant, and make interpretations about the text as a whole.	You spell and punctuate with consistent accuracy, and use a very wide range of vocabulary and sentence structures to achieve effective control of meaning.	
Good to High	**A thoughtful, detailed response with well-chosen references.** At the top end, you address all aspects of the task in a clearly expressed way, and examine key aspects in detail. You are beginning to consider implications, explore alternative interpretations or ideas; at the top end, you do this fairly regularly and with some confidence.	You spell and punctuate with considerable accuracy, and use a considerable range of vocabulary and sentence structures to achieve general control of meaning.	
Mid	**A consistent response with clear understanding of the main ideas shown.** You use a range of references to support your ideas and your viewpoint is logical and easy to follow. Some evidence of commenting on writers' effects though more needed.	You spell and punctuate with reasonable accuracy, and use a reasonable range of vocabulary and sentence structures.	
Lower	**Some relevant ideas but an inconsistent and rather simple response in places.** You show you have understood the task and you make some points to support what you say, but the evidence is not always well chosen. Your analysis is a bit basic and you do not comment in much detail on the writer's methods.	Your spelling and punctuation are inconsistent and your vocabulary and sentence structures are both limited. Some of these make your meaning unclear.	